Jesus, Keep Me Near the Cross

Experiencing the Passion and Power of Easter

EDITED BY
NANCY GUTHRIE

CROSSWAY BOOKS

WHEATON, ILLINOIS

Design and typesetting: Lakeside Design Plus
Cover design: Jon McGrath
Cover illustration: Art Resource Inc.
First printing 2009
Printed in the United States of America

Chapters 10 and 13 Scripture quotations are from *The New American Standard Bible®*. Copyright © The Lockman Foundation 1960, 1962, 1963, 1968, 1971, 1972, 1973, 1975, 1977, 1995. Used by permission.

Chapters 1, 7, 8, 12, 19, and 21 Scripture quotations are from the *King James Version* of the Bible.

Chapter opening quotations and chapters 2, 4, and 6 Scripture quotations are from *The Holy Bible, English Standard Version®*, copyright © 2001 by Crossway Bibles, a publishing ministry of Good News Publishers. Used by permission. All rights reserved.

Chapters 3, 5, 9, 11, 14, 16, 17, 20, 23, and 24 Scripture quotations are from *The Holy Bible: New International Version®*. Copyright © 1973, 1978, 1984 by International Bible Society. Used by permission of Zondervan Publishing House. All rights reserved.

The "NIV" and "New International Version" trademarks are registered in the United States Patent and Trademark Office by International Bible Society. Use of either trademark requires the permission of International Bible Society.

Chapters 15 and 25 Scripture quotations are from *The New King James Version*. Copyright © 1982, Thomas Nelson, Inc. Used by permission.

Chapter 18 Scripture quotations are from *The Revised Standard Version*. Copyright © 1946, 1952, 1971, 1973 by the Division of Christian Education of the National Council of the Churches of Christ in the U.S.A.

All emphases in Scripture quotations have been added by the authors.

Trade Paperback ISBN: 978-1-4335-0181-4

Library of Congress Cataloging-in-Publication Data
Jesus, keep me near the cross : experiencing the passion and power of Easter / edited by Nancy Guthrie.
    p. cm.
  Includes bibliographical references.
  ISBN 978-1-4335-0181-4 (tpb)
  1. Easter—Meditations. 2. Jesus Christ—Crucifixion—Meditations. 3. Jesus Christ—Resurrection—Meditations. I. Guthrie, Nancy.
BV55.J38 2009
232.96—dc22

                                                        2008028618

BP   17   16   15   14   13   12   11   10   09
             9   8   7   6   5   4   3   2

I fondly dedicate this book to Estelle Hudgins Teeter, my sixth grade Sunday school teacher who took an interest in me, invested in me, and is still teaching me with her selfless life.

Estelle, I saw in you a radiant joy in knowing Christ, the power of his resurrection, and the fellowship of sharing in his sufferings, becoming like him. . . .
You made me want to love Jesus like you do.

Praying that you will love Jesus with a radiant joy.

May thy cross be to me
as the tree that sweetens my bitter Marahs,
as the rod that blossoms with life and beauty,
as the brazen serpent that calls forth the look
    of faith.
By thy cross crucify my every sin;
Use it to increase my intimacy with thyself;
Make it the ground of all my comfort,
    the liveliness of all my duties,
    the sum of all thy gospel promises,
    the comfort of all my afflictions,
    the vigour of my love, thankfulness, graces,
    the very essence of my religion;
And by it give me that rest without rest,
    the rest of ceaseless praise.

—The Valley of Vision

CONTENTS

Preface   9

1. True Contemplation of the Cross   11
   Martin Luther

2. He Set His Face to Go to Jerusalem   15
   John Piper

3. An Innocent Man Crushed by God   21
   Alistair Begg

4. The Cup   27
   C. J. Mahaney

5. Gethsemane   31
   R. Kent Hughes

6. Betrayed, Denied, Deserted   37
   J. Ligon Duncan III

7. Then Did They Spit in His Face   43
   Charles Spurgeon

8. The Silence of the Lamb   49
   Adrian Rogers

9. The Sufferings of Christ   55
   J. C. Ryle

10. Father, Forgive Them   61
    John MacArthur

11. With Loud Cries and Tears   67
    John Owen
12. That He Might Destroy the Works of the Devil   75
    Martyn Lloyd-Jones
13. I Am Thirsty   81
    Joseph "Skip" Ryan
14. God-Forsaken   85
    Philip Graham Ryken
15. Cursed   91
    R. C. Sproul
16. Into Your Hands I Commit My Spirit   97
    James Montgomery Boice
17. Blood and Water   101
    John Calvin
18. He Descended into Hell and Ascended into Heaven   105
    J. I. Packer
19. A Sweet-Smelling Savor to God   111
    Jonathan Edwards
20. The Most Important Word in the Universe   115
    Raymond C. Ortlund Jr.
21. Resurrection Preview   121
    Francis Schaeffer
22. Peace Be unto You   127
    Saint Augustine
23. Knowing the Power of His Resurrection   131
    Tim Keller
24. Sharing His Sufferings   139
    Joni Eareckson Tada
25. Crucified with Christ   145
    Stephen F. Olford

    Notes   151

PREFACE

"For the word of the cross is folly to those who are perishing, but to us who are being saved it is the power of God."

1 Corinthians 1:18

I've often found myself in churches that made more of Mother's Day than Palm Sunday, with little focus given to entering into the passion of Jesus in an intentional and meaningful way as Easter approached. Too many years I've found that I have rushed from Palm Sunday into Easter morning, from palm branches to the empty tomb, without giving my mind and my heart over to thoughtful contemplation of the cross. If you can relate to my lament, then I hope you will join me as we turn our gaze toward the cross through the pages of this book.

Oh, what we miss out on when we rush past the cross of Christ. Oh, the richness and reward when we stop to linger before it, when we take the time to "consider him who endured from sinners such hostility against himself" (Heb. 12:3). In a culture where crosses have become commonplace as architecture and jewelry, how we need to truly gaze upon the cross of Christ in all of its ugliness and beauty, in its death and in its healing, in the painful price paid there, and in its free gift of grace. *Jesus, keep us near the cross.*

9

In the pages that follow, gifted theologians and Bible teachers will help us to stop and linger at the cross. I've drawn from the writings and sermons of classic and contemporary writers and teachers to create meditations that will draw us into an experience of the passion of the cross and the power of the resurrection.

How we need to have our hearts broken again by our sin that put Jesus on the cross. How we need to have our confidence grounded by what Jesus accomplished on the cross. And how we need to have our hope anchored in the promise of resurrection. I pray that is what you will experience as you read this book. May Jesus draw you and keep you near his cross.

Nancy Guthrie

1

⚜RUE ⚜ONTEMPLATION
OF THE ⚜ROSS

Martin Luther

"Looking to Jesus, the founder and perfecter of our faith, who for the joy that was set before him endured the cross, despising the shame, and is seated at the right hand of the throne of God. Consider him who endured from sinners such hostility against himself, so that you may not grow weary or fainthearted."

Hebrews 12:2–3

et us meditate a moment on the passion of Christ. Some do so falsely in that they merely rail against Judas and the Jews. Some carry crucifixes to protect themselves from water, fire, and sword, and turn the suffering of Christ into an amulet against suffering. Some weep, and that is the end of it. The true contemplation is that in which the heart is crushed and the conscience smitten. You must be overwhelmed by the frightful wrath of God who so hated sin that he spared not his only begotten

Son. What can the sinner expect if the beloved Son was so afflicted? It must be an inexpressible and unendurable yearning that causes God's Son himself so to suffer. Ponder this and you will tremble, and the more you ponder, the deeper you will tremble.

Take this to heart and doubt not that you are the one who killed Christ. Your sins certainly did, and when you see the nails driven through his hands, be sure that you are pounding, and when the thorns pierce his brow, know that they are your evil thoughts. Consider that if one thorn pierced Christ you deserve one hundred thousand.

The whole value of the meditation of the suffering of Christ lies in this, that man should come to the knowledge of himself and sink and tremble. If you are so hardened that you do not tremble, then you have reason to tremble. Pray to God that he may soften your heart and make fruitful your meditation upon the suffering of Christ, for we of ourselves are incapable of proper reflection unless God instills it.

But if one does meditate rightly on the suffering of Christ for a day, an hour, or even a quarter of an hour, this we may confidently say is better than a whole year of fasting, days of psalm singing, yes, than even one hundred masses, because this reflection changes the whole man and makes him new, as once he was in baptism.

If, then, Christ is so firmly planted in your heart, and if you are become an enemy to sin out of love and not fear, then henceforth the suffering of Christ, which began as a sacrament, may continue lifelong as an example. When tribulation and sickness assail you, think how slight these are compared to the thorns and the nails of Christ. If you are thwarted, remember how he was bound and dragged. If pride besets you, see how the Lord was mocked and with robbers despised. If unchastity incites your flesh, recall how his flesh was scourged, pierced, and smitten. If hate, envy, and vengeance tempt you, think how Christ for you and all his enemies interceded with tears, though he might rather have avenged himself. If you are afflicted and cannot have your way, take heart and say, "Why should I not suffer when my Lord sweat blood for very anguish?"

Astounding it is that the cross of Christ has so fallen into forgetfulness, for is it not forgetfulness of the cross when no one wishes to suffer but rather to enjoy himself and evade the cross? You must personally experience suffering with Christ. He suffered for your sake, and should you not suffer for his sake, as well as for your own?

Two texts in the Old Testament apply to Christ. The first is, "Thou art fairer than the children of men" (Ps. 45:2), and the second is, "He hath no form nor comeliness" (Isa. 53:2). Evidently these passages must be understood in differing sense. To the eyes of the flesh, he was the lowest among the sons of men, a derision, and to the eyes of the spirit there was none fairer than he. The eyes of the flesh cannot see this. What, then is the nature of this beauty? It is wisdom and love, light for the understanding, and power for the soul, for in suffering and dying Christ displayed all the wisdom and the truth with which the understanding can be adorned. All the treasures of wisdom and knowledge are hidden in him, and they are hidden because they are visible only to the eye of the spirit.

The whole value of the meditation of the suffering of Christ lies in this, that man should come to the knowledge of himself and sink and tremble.

The greater and the more wonderful is the excellence of his love by contrast with the lowliness of his form, the hate and pain of passion. Herein we come to know both God and ourselves. His beauty is his own, and through it we learn to know him. His uncomeliness and passion are ours, and in them we know ourselves, for what he suffered in the flesh, we must inwardly suffer in the spirit. He has in truth borne our stripes. Here, then, in an unspeakably clear mirror you see yourself. You must know that through your sins you are as uncomely and mangled as you see him here.

If we consider the persons, we ought to suffer a thousand and again a thousand times more than Christ because he is God and we are dust and ashes, yet it is the reverse. He who had a thousand and again a thousand times less need, has taken upon himself a thousand and again a thousand times more than we. No understanding can fathom nor tongue can express, no writing can record, but only the inward feeling can grasp what is involved in the suffering of Christ.

Adapted from *Martin Luther's Easter Book*, edited by Roland H. Bainton. Copyright © 1962 by W. L. Jenkins. Used by permission of the estate of Roland Bainton.

Scripture quotations are from the *King James Version* of the Bible.

2

᛫ᚻᛖ ᛋᛖᛏ ᚻᛁᛋ ᚠᚪᚳᛖ TO ᚷᛟ TO ᛃᛖᚱᚢᛋᚪᛚᛖᛗ
John Piper

"When the days drew near for him to be taken up, he set his face to go to Jerusalem."

Luke 9:51

 uke describes the arrival of Jesus in Jerusalem at the be-
ginning of that last week of his earthly life:

As he was drawing near—already on the way down the Mount of
Olives—the whole multitude of his disciples began to rejoice and
praise God with a loud voice for all the mighty works that they had
seen, saying, "Blessed is the King who comes in the name of the Lord!
Peace in heaven and glory in the highest!" (Luke 19:37–38)

There is no doubt what was in the disciples' minds. This was the
fulfillment of Zechariah's prophecy given centuries earlier:

Rejoice greatly, O daughter of Zion!
Shout aloud, O daughter of Jerusalem!
Behold, your king is coming to you;
righteous and having salvation is he,
humble and mounted on a donkey,
on a colt, the foal of a donkey.
I will cut off the chariot from Ephraim
and the war horse from Jerusalem;
and the battle bow shall be cut off,
and he shall speak peace to the nations;
his rule shall be from sea to sea,
and from the River to the ends of the earth. (Zech. 9:9–10)

The long-awaited Messiah had come, the king of Israel, and not just of Israel but of all the earth. Jerusalem would be his capital city. From here he would rule the world in peace and righteousness. What a day this was! How their hearts must have pounded in their chests! And must not their hands have been sweaty like warriors in readiness just before the bugle sounds the battle! . . .

To be sure the disciples' understanding of Jesus' kingship at this point is flawed. But hastening events will correct that soon enough. In essence they are correct. Jesus is the king of Israel, and the kingdom he is inaugurating will bring peace to all the nations and spread from sea to sea. The book of Revelation pictures the final fulfillment of Palm Sunday in the age to come like this:

I looked, and behold, a great multitude that no man could number, from every nation, from all tribes and peoples and languages, standing before the throne and before the Lamb, clothed in white robes, with palm branches in their hands, and crying out with a loud voice, "Salvation belongs to our God who sits on the throne, and to the Lamb!" (Rev. 7:9–10)

The entry into Jerusalem with waving palms (John 12:13) was a short-lived preview of the eternal Palm Sunday to come. It needed to be said. If the disciples hadn't said it, the rocks would have.

But if Jesus had taken his throne on that first day of palms, none of us would ever be robed in white or waving palms of praise in the age to come. There had to be the cross, and that is what the disciples had not yet understood.

Back in Luke 9, as Jesus prepared to set out for Jerusalem from Galilee, he tried to explain this to his disciples. In verse 22 he said, "The Son of Man must suffer many things and be rejected by the elders and chief priests and scribes, and be killed, and on the third day be raised." And in verse 44 he told them, "Let these words sink into your ears: The Son of Man is about to be delivered into the hands of men." But verse 45 tells us, "They did not understand this saying, and it was concealed from them, so that they might not perceive it. And they were afraid to ask him about this saying." Therefore, their understanding of Jesus' last journey to Jerusalem was flawed. They saw him as a king moving in to take control. And he was. But they could not grasp that the victory Jesus would win in Jerusalem over sin and Satan and death and all the enemies of righteousness and joy—that this victory would be won through his own horrible suffering and death; and that the kingdom which they thought would be established immediately (Luke 19:11) would, in fact, be thousands of years in coming.

And their misunderstanding of Jesus' journey to Jerusalem results in a misunderstanding of the meaning of discipleship. This is why this is important for us to see, lest we make the same mistake.

In Luke 9:51 we read, "When the days drew near for him to be taken up, he set his face to go to Jerusalem." To set his face toward Jerusalem meant something very different for Jesus than it did for the disciples. You can see the visions of greatness that danced in their heads in verse 46: "An argument arose among them as to which of them was the greatest." Jerusalem and glory were just around the corner. O what it would mean when Jesus took the throne!

But Jesus had another vision in his head. One wonders how he carried it all alone and so long. Jerusalem meant one thing for Jesus: certain death.

He was under no illusions of a quick and heroic death. He predicted in Luke 18:31–33, "See, we are going up to Jerusalem, and everything that is written of the Son of Man by the prophets will be accomplished. For he will be delivered over to the Gentiles and will be mocked and shamefully treated and spit upon. And after flogging him, they will kill him. . . ." When Jesus set his face to go to Jerusalem, he set his face to die. . . .

Jesus' journey to Jerusalem is our journey, and if he set his face to go there and die, we must set our face to die with him.

If we were to look at Jesus' death merely as a result of a betrayer's deceit and the Sanhedrin's envy and Pilate's spinelessness and the soldiers' nails and spear, it might seem very involuntary. And the benefit of salvation that comes to us who believe from this death might be viewed as God's way of making a virtue out of a necessity. But once you read Luke 9:51 all such thoughts vanish. Jesus was not accidentally entangled in a web of injustice. The saving benefits of his death for sinners were not an afterthought. God planned it all out of infinite love to sinners like us and appointed a time. Jesus, who was the very embodiment of his Father's love for sinners, saw that the time had come and set his face to fulfill his mission: to die in Jerusalem for our sake. "No one takes [my life] from me [he said], but I lay it down of my own accord . . ." (John 10:18). . . .

Here is a question put to every believer by this text: does discipleship mean deploying God's missiles against the enemy in righteous indignation? Or does discipleship mean following him on the Calvary road which leads to suffering and death? The answer of the whole New Testament is this: the surprise about Jesus the Messiah is that he came to live a life of sacrificial, dying service before he comes a second time to reign in glory. And the surprise about discipleship is that it demands a life of sacrificial, dying service before we can reign with Christ in glory.

Jerusalem meant one thing for Jesus: certain death.

Jesus' journey to Jerusalem is our journey, and if he set his face to go there and die, we must set our face to die with him.

One might be tempted to reason in just the opposite way: that since Jesus suffered so much and died in our place, therefore, we are free to go straight to the head of the class, as it were, and skip all the exams. He suffered so we could have comfort. He died so we could live. He bore abuse so we could be esteemed. He gave up the treasures of heaven so we could lay up treasures on earth. He brought the kingdom and paid for our entrance, and now we live in it with all its earthly privileges. But all this is not biblical reasoning. It goes against the plain teaching in this very context. Luke 9:23–24 reads: "If anyone would come after me, let him deny himself and take up his cross daily and follow me. For whoever would save his life will lose it, but whoever loses his life for my sake will save it."

When Jesus set his face to walk the Calvary road, he was not merely taking our place; he was setting our pattern. He is substitute and pacesetter. If we seek to secure our life through returning evil for evil or surrounding ourselves with luxury in the face of human need, we will lose our life. We can save our life only if we follow Christ on the Calvary road.

Adapted from "He Set His Face to Go to Jerusalem," sermon by John Piper, Bethlehem Baptist Church, Minneapolis, April 4, 1982. The complete text of this sermon is available at: http://www.desiring-god.org/ResourceLibrary/Sermons/ByDate/1982/339_He_Set_His_Face_to_Go_to_Jerusalem/. Used by permission.

Scripture quotations are from *The Holy Bible, English Standard Version*®.

3

An Innocent Man Crushed by God

Alistair Begg

"For our sake he made him to be sin who knew no sin, so that in him we might become the righteousness of God."

2 Corinthians 5:21

y soul is overwhelmed with sorrow to the point of death," Jesus said (Mark 14:34). It was not that he turned a corner in the road and was confronted by something that took him unawares. He had been moving purposely toward this event. Indeed, from all of eternity the Father, the Son, and the Spirit in a covenant of redemption had planned what each of them would do. And Jesus, in light of this, had been moving inexorably toward Jerusalem. He had "set his face to go to Jerusalem."

In John's gospel, he records Jesus saying to his father, "Now my heart is troubled, and what shall I say? 'Father, save me from

this hour'? No, it was for this very reason I came to this hour"
(John 12:27).

Now, in the familiar setting of the Mount of Olives, having gone
out as usual with his disciples following, Jesus is engulfed by pent
up emotions. Suddenly everything that he has considered before
him comes into his human psychology and
grips him with immense passion. We know
that because we find him crying earnestly and
sweating profusely.

*Jesus, the beloved
and precious
to the Father,
is about to be
destroyed at the
hands of God.*

What makes this a drama of compassion?
The nature of what he is about to do.
The time had come for Jesus to surrender himself as an eternal expiatory sacrifice for sin.
Jesus was about to bow himself into the hands of his enemies, about
to be condemned and crucified. Jesus, the beloved and precious to
the Father, is about to be destroyed at the hands of God.

Three verses help us to grasp the reality of what is happening here.

Isaiah 53:10: "Yet it was the LORD's will to crush him and cause
him to suffer."

Romans 8:32: "He who did not spare his own Son, but gave him
up for us all—"

2 Corinthians 5:21: "God made him who had no sin to be sin for
us, so that in him we might become the righteousness of God."

This is beyond belief. An innocent man is about to be crushed
by God. An innocent man is being delivered up by God to be
sacrificed. An innocent man is being made sin on behalf of
others.

Now when we read our Bibles and think about these things, it is not wrong to say that in the cross the love of God is declared. But to say that does not get to the depth of it. It is right to say Jesus is our priest and our representative, but even that does not get to the heart of what is happening here. It is right to say that Jesus died on our behalf, that he identified himself with us. But all of that terminology still falls short of the absolute nature of what is taking place in the passion of Christ.

Because here our advocate does not simply end up in the courtroom, he ends up on the cross.

On a daily basis we see courtroom scenes on the news of people on trial for various crimes. We see the defendant accompanied by his advocate or lawyer. Can you imagine turning on CNN and the roles are reversed? Can you imagine seeing the lawyer or advocate on trial for the crime his client committed? Or even more incredible, can you imagine that a judgment of guilty is made and the death penalty is meted out and it is the attorney who dies and not the defendant? That would be bizarre. It would be immoral. It would be wrong, because the attorney didn't do anything.

But that's what we see in Jesus as our sinless Advocate receives the punishment we, who are guilty, deserve.

It wasn't that Jesus simply stepped up and said, "I'll do this for you." It is that Jesus became the very embodiment of all that sin is.

Jesus is our high priest, but what kind of priest is this who becomes the sacrifice? Priests *offer* sacrifices—but this priest *is* the sacrifice. This priest lays himself on the altar.

You see, Jesus died for sin—but not for his own sin. He had no sin. He was in every sense *made sin* for us. He became all of our rebellion, all of our lying, all of our cheating, all of our adultery, all of our filth, all of our ugliness. He became all of that on the cross. Otherwise, how could God crucify his Son? It wasn't that Jesus simply stepped up and said, "I'll do this for you." It is that Jesus became the very embodiment of all that sin is.

Without substitution the death of Jesus is unintelligible. Unless what we have here is what is being described in 2 Corinthians 5:21, that he was *made sin* for us—not that he was made *a sinner* for us—but *made sin* for us, then how else do you explain it? What possible justification could God have for crucifying the innocent unless in substitution he became all that we are in our sin and rebellion in order that, in the mastery and mystery of his grace, in him we might become the very righteousness of God?

> And when I think that God, his Son not sparing, sent him to
>   die, I scarce can take it in,
> That on the cross, my burden gladly bearing, he bled and died
>   to take away my sin.[1]

He goes to the garbage heap for all my garbage. He goes to the cross for all my rebellion, for all my filthy thoughts, all my selfish preoccupation, all my pride, all my self-aggrandizement.

> Bearing shame and scoffing rude
> In my place condemned he stood.[2]

There is no story in all of human history like this. There is no notion in all religions of the world that comes close to touching this. This is imponderable, mysterious, majestic, glorious. This is all about God and the wonder of his grace.

As Jesus faced this awesome prospect, he brings his disciples close and says, "My soul is overwhelmed to the point of death."

When the lights come on for the disciples after the resurrection, they realize that in the cross Jesus was substituting himself for us, changing places with us, taking the guilt of our sin to himself, accepting divine judgment that is justly and rightly against us.

In the cross God does two things, which would be otherwise impossible.

First, he pardons those who believe in Christ. Although they have sinned and deserve only condemnation, he pardons sinners. How can a just God pardon sinners? Only because all of our sin was transferred to Christ. This lays the ax at the roots of every religious person's endeavors to make himself acceptable to God by trying harder, attending more, praying more intensely—as if by some mechanism, we might be able to tip the scales in our favor.

God pardons sinners even though they have sinned and sinned and deserve only condemnation. And if he didn't, we would be forever excluded from his presence.

Second, he displays and satisfies his perfect, holy justice by executing the punishment our sins deserve. Without this God would not be true to himself.

Here's the gospel in a phrase. Because Christ died for us, those who trust in him may know that their guilt has been pardoned once and for all.

What will we have to say before the bar of God's judgment? Only one thing. Christ died in my place. That's the gospel.

Adapted from "Jesus Our Substitute," sermon by Alistair Begg, Parkside Church, Chagrin Falls, Ohio, July 13, 2003. Used by permission.

Scripture references are from *The Holy Bible: New International Version*®.

4

𝕿HE 𝕮UP

C. J. Mahaney

"And going a little farther he fell on his face and prayed, saying, 'My Father, if it be possible, let this cup pass from me; nevertheless, not as I will, but as you will.'"

Matthew 26:39

s Jesus lies prostrate on the ground, we overhear him praying: "Abba, Father, all things are possible for you. Remove this cup from me. Yet not what I will, but what you will."

He's making this plea repeatedly. With his face to the ground, we can see sweat on his temples. He lifts his head, and his expression reveals an agony so intense that his sweat is "like great drops of blood falling down to the ground."

His words tell us why: "Remove this *cup*," Jesus pleads again. In this moment, there's no doubt what is dominating his heart and mind.

27

What is this cup? It is clearly a reference to the wrath of God for your sins and mine.

If we knew the Scriptures as Jesus does—Scriptures that no doubt have been much on his mind in these hours—we couldn't escape this reference. Isaiah 51:17 shows us this cup in God's extended hand—it's "the cup of his wrath," and for those who drink from it, it's "the cup of staggering." This cup contains the full vehemence and fierceness of God's holy wrath poured out against all sin, and we discover in Scripture that it's intended for all of sinful humanity to drink. It's your cup . . . and mine.

In the vivid imagery of the Old Testament, this cup is filled with "fire and sulfur and a scorching wind" like some volcanic firestorm, like all the fury of the Mount St. Helens eruption concentrated within a coffee mug. No wonder Scripture says that tasting from this cup causes the drinker to "stagger and be crazed." No wonder that when Jesus stares into the detestable vessel, he stumbles to the ground.

That's why there's shuddering terror and deep distress for him at this moment. In the crucible of human weakness he's brought face to face with the abhorrent reality of bearing our iniquity and becoming the object of God's full and furious wrath.

What Jesus recoils from here is not an anticipation of the physical pain associated with crucifixion. Rather it's a pain infinitely greater—the agony of being abandoned by his Father.

As one Bible commentator notes, Jesus entered the garden "to be with the Father for an interlude before his betrayal, but found Hell rather than Heaven open before him."[1] Knowing the hour for his death is fast approaching, Jesus has come here in need as never before of his Father's comfort and strength. Instead, hell—utter separation from God—is thrust in his face.

We hear him cry out: Father—is there an alternative? Is there any way to avoid this? If there's a way this could pass from me, would you please provide that alternative?

Silence. We can see it in his face—Jesus received no answer to this desperate entreaty.

A second time, then again a third, he pleads for an alternative to that horror of abandonment by his Father. *If* such an alternative existed, the Father would most surely provide it. But the obedient Son's plea to his loving Father is met with silence. Why?

Listen to this verse for the very first time: *For God so loved the world . . .* that he's silent at this moment when his Son appeals for an alternative.

This is what bearing our sin means to *him*—utter distress of soul as he confronts total abandonment and absolute wrath from his Father on the cross, a distress and an abandonment and a rejection we cannot begin to grasp.

What Jesus recoils from here is not an anticipation of the physical pain associated with crucifixion. Rather it's a pain infinitely greater—the agony of being abandoned by his Father.

In this, our Savior's darkest hour . . . do you recognize his love for you?

Listen again to the precious and powerful words we hear him repeat to his Father:

"Yet not what I will, but what you will."

"Yet not what I will, but what you will."

"Yet not what I will, but what you will."

Jesus is saying, "Father, I willingly drink this cup by your command—I'll drink it all."

And he will. He'll drink all of it, leaving not a drop.

Not only will he leave nothing in that cup of wrath for us to drink . . . but today you and I find ourselves with another cup in our hands. It's the cup of salvation. From this precious new cup we find ourselves drinking and drinking—drinking consistently, drinking endlessly, drinking eternally . . . for the cup of salvation is always full and overflowing. We can drink from this cup only because Jesus spoke those words about the other cup: "Yet not what I will, but what you will."

Today you and I find ourselves with another cup in our hands. It's the cup of salvation.

I will drink it all.

As we watch Jesus pray in agony in Gethsemane, he has every right to turn his tearful eyes toward you and me and shout, "This is *your* cup. *You're* responsible for this. It's *your* sin! *You* drink it." This cup should rightfully be thrust into my hand and yours.

Instead, Jesus freely takes it himself . . . so that from the cross he can look down at you and me, whisper our names and say, "I drain this cup for you—for you who have lived in defiance of me, who have hated me, who have opposed me. I drink it all . . . for *you.*"

Excerpted from *Christ Our Mediator* by C. J. Mahaney. Copyright © 2004 by Sovereign Grace Ministries. Used by permission of WaterBrook Multnomah Publishing Group, a division of Random House, Inc.

Scripture quotations are from *The Holy Bible, English Standard Version*®.

5

GETHSEMANE

R. Kent Hughes

"When Jesus had spoken these words, he went out with his disciples across the Kidron Valley, where there was a garden, which he and his disciples entered."

John 18:1

he Lord deliberately chose Gethsemane. John's specific mention of it as a "garden" in John 18:1 suggests that the apostle has in mind a deliberate comparison with the original garden of Eden. The symbolism is this:

- The first Adam began life in a garden. Christ, the second Adam, came at the end of his life to a garden.
- In Eden Adam sinned. In Gethsemane the Savior overcame sin.
- In Eden Adam fell. In Gethsemane Jesus conquered.
- In Eden Adam hid himself. In Gethsemane our Lord boldly presented himself.

- In Eden the sword was drawn. In Gethsemane it was sheathed.

This symbolism is not accidental or incidental to Jesus' death. It was an assurance for future generations of readers that Christ was in control.

Enhancing this symbolism, John mentions in verse 1 that "Jesus left with his disciples and crossed the Kidron Valley." A drain ran from the temple altar down to the Kidron ravine to drain away the blood of sacrifices. At this time of year more than two hundred thousand lambs were slain. So when Jesus and his band crossed the Kidron, it was red with the blood of sacrifice.[1] This divine poetry shows that what was about to take place was not beyond the control of God, regardless of how it appeared.

An unspeakable horror overcame Christ in Gethsemane as he wrestled with the reality of what was to come. He experienced intense agony: "And he began to be sorrowful and troubled. Then he said to them, 'My soul is overwhelmed with sorrow to the point of death . . .'" (Matt. 26:37–38). Mark tells us that Christ repeatedly (literal translation) fell to the ground "and prayed that if possible the hour might pass from him" (Mark 14:35). Evidently he was in such agony that he would cast himself to the ground, then stand up, then again fall to the ground in prayer. No one has known the sorrow our Lord experienced. Luke the physician says, "And being in anguish, he prayed more earnestly, and his sweat was like drops of blood falling to the ground" (Luke 22:44). So great was his agony as the coming dread engulfed him that he actually broke out in a bloody sweat. These and similar verses caused Celsus, a second-century heretic, and others after him to argue that Christ

The under-standing of what the sacrifice meant, which only omniscience could bring, caused our Lord to break out in a bloody sweat.

was only a man. After all, they reasoned, he displayed in the garden and on the cross less fortitude than other men have shown in battle or at the stake.

But actually Christ's agony demonstrates that he knew exactly what was involved. It was not the pain that caused the horror. It was not the shame. It was not the imminent desertion of the disciples. It was the fact that he was going to pay the penalty for our sins! The understanding of what the sacrifice meant, which only omniscience could bring, caused our Lord to break out in a bloody sweat. It was the crushing realization of the horror that crushed him. Christ's resolve to endure the agony, even at such a great price, demonstrates his lordship and divinity.

John picks up the narrative after Jesus' formal resolve to drink the cup. The moments are loaded with drama:

> Now Judas, who betrayed him, knew the place, because Jesus had often met there with his disciples. So Judas came to the grove, guiding a detachment of soldiers and some officials from the chief priests and Pharisees. They were carrying torches, lanterns and weapons. (John 18:2–3)

It was the middle of a spring night, and it was probably cloudless because John mentions it was "cold" (v. 18). The ancient olive trees cast eerie shadows across the encampment. Beyond the ravine lay the scattered lights of Jerusalem, where Judas had earlier made his rendezvous with the Roman cohort of six hundred men from the Tower of Antonia. Matthew later described that cohort as "a large crowd" (Matt. 26:47). The soldiers of the cohort were fully armed, each carrying a short sword. With them came the temple guards with their clubs. Jews and Gentiles were for once united in a common cause. They had carefully chosen the time and place. They wanted to arrest Jesus away from the people, so there would be no riot, but they were prepared for the worst. The sight must have been terrifying as the long line, punctuated by the flickering torches, wound down from the dark, high walls of the Holy City, across the stained Kidron, and up the slopes of Olivet toward the garden. No doubt Judas was in the lead. In a few minutes he would, as Mark says, "fervently kiss" the Master as a sign of betrayal (Mark 14:45, literal Greek).

Our Lord, instead of waiting to be found, went forward to meet the armed crowd. In response to their question, he openly identified himself. Their reaction was to fall to the ground. John represents their response as a miracle. They do not fall down when he asked them what they wanted, but only after he said, "I am he" or literally "I am." I do not agree with those who partially explain this response by pointing to the moral force that some great and good men and women possess. The Roman soldiers knew nothing of Jesus and had no reason to fear him. Jesus answered in the style of deity, using the divine title, I AM, going back to the burning bush of Exodus 3 when God said, "I AM WHO I AM" (v. 14). Jesus' response was the last exercise of the power by which he calmed the seas, stilled the winds, and healed the sick. Was Jesus caught on the wheel of history? Hardly! He is the axis of history. In a very real sense the cohort did not arrest Jesus—he arrested them! His words were a gracious warning that they were in way over their heads. Christ could have called ten thousand angels, each sixty feet high and armed with laser beams. But he did not:

> I lay down my life—only to take it up again. No one takes it from me, but I lay it down of my own accord. I have authority to lay it down and authority to take it up again. . . . (John 10:17–18)

Apparently Judas's betrayal of the Messiah with a kiss was just too much for Peter (cf. Luke 22:48–50). Out came his hidden short sword, and he lunged at Malchus, his sword coming down hard on Malchus's helmet and bouncing down the side, lopping off his right ear. Our primal instincts rejoice that at least one blow was struck for Jesus. The truth is, though, Peter's rash action could have destroyed the church. Calvin comments: "No thanks to him that Christ was not kept from death and that his name was not a perpetual disgrace."[2] Imagine the pounding tension as Malchus stood wide-eyed, blood pouring through his fingers, a hundred steel blades ringing from their scabbards in gruesome symphony. Then came Jesus' words (Luke 22:51): "No more of this!" Then he touched Malchus's ear and healed him. Not only is our Lord powerful and gracious, but he is merciful, even in his final moments.

We could not have paid for our own sins even if we were punished for them for all eternity.

Finally, note the Lord's majestic summary statement: "Shall I not drink the cup the Father has given me?" (John 18:11). The "cup" was the cross, the cup of judgment that we should have drunk. Jesus took upon himself our punishment in those hours of darkness on the cross. We could not have paid for our own sins even if we were punished for them for all eternity.

> Death and the curse were in that cup,
> Oh Christ, 'twas full for Thee;
> But Thou hast drained the last dark dregs,
> 'Tis empty now for me.

Earlier Jesus had wrestled with the terror of the cup, saying: "Not my will, but yours be done." Now he sovereignly says, "Shall I not drink it?"

The surroundings of Christ's final hour clearly displayed his sovereign control. The intensity of his agony and his sovereign resolve to bear it, his control over his captors, his protection of his own, his grace to the wounded, all proved he is an omniscient, all-powerful God. Christ was in control when life was falling in, when things looked the worst.

How does this relate to us? Though Christ's Gethsemane was infinitely beyond human experience, Gethsemanes are a part of believers' lives.

Gethsemane was not a tragedy, and neither are our Gethsemanes. This does not do away with the wounds of affliction in this life, but it is encouraging to see that behind human tragedy stands the benevolent and wise purpose of the Lord of human history. Life may be dark at times, tragedy may come, and at times the whole world may seem to be falling apart. The wheel may appear ready to crush us. But this is not the end. "And we know that in all things God works for the good of those who love him, who have been called according to his purpose" (Rom. 8:28), even in Gethsemane.

Excerpted from *John: That You May Believe* by R. Kent Hughes. Copyright © 1999 by R. Kent Hughes. Used by permission of Crossway Books.

Scripture references are from *The Holy Bible: New International Version*®.

6

ᏴETRAYED, ᎠENIED, ᎠESERTED

J. Ligon Duncan III

"While he was still speaking, Judas came, one of the twelve, and with him a great crowd with swords and clubs, from the chief priests and the elders of the people. Now the betrayer had given them a sign, saying, 'The one I will kiss is the man; seize him.' And he came up to Jesus at once and said, 'Greetings, Rabbi!' And he kissed him. Jesus said to him, 'Friend, do what you came to do.' Then they came up and laid hands on Jesus and seized him. And behold, one of those who were with Jesus stretched out his hand and drew his sword and struck the servant of the high priest and cut off his ear. Then Jesus said to him, 'Put your sword back into its place. For all who take the sword will perish by the sword. Do you think that I cannot appeal to my Father, and he will at once send me more than twelve legions of angels? But how then should the Scriptures be fulfilled, that it must be so?' At that hour Jesus said to the crowds, 'Have you come out as against a robber, with swords and clubs to capture me? Day after day I sat in the temple teaching, and you did not seize me. But all this has taken place that the Scriptures of the prophets might be fulfilled.' Then all the disciples left him and fled."

Matthew 26:47–56

s everything is falling apart before his eyes, Jesus shows an incredible display of his character and his calmness in the midst of his betrayal.

Jesus and his disciples are approached by Judas and the crowd, and Judas identifies Jesus to the soldiers by kissing him. Greeting with a kiss was a normal way in the Near East to affectionately greet one another. This affectionate sign heightens the despicableness of what Judas has done. He has used a sign of affection to mark Jesus for arrest. The manner by which Judas betrays Jesus emphasizes the bitterness and despicable nature of this crime. Hendriksen beautifully says they came with torches and lanterns to seek out the Light of the world. They came with swords and clubs to subdue the Prince of Peace![1]

Jesus, however, does something absolutely mind-boggling. He basically gives Judas and this mob permission to arrest him. "Friend," he says, "do what you have come to do. Go ahead and get it over with." Jesus is showing his sovereignty over these circumstances. His character, his resolution, and his majesty are brought into bold relief against a backdrop of this betrayal.

Crises have a way of revealing our character. In the midst of a trial, we sometimes learn things about ourselves that we would rather not know. At other times we see friends really rise to the occasion in the midst of trial.

Jesus' character shines through in this moment of crisis. Don Carson says, "In all of the various trials and mockery that Jesus underwent, His character stood out more and more clearly against the backdrop of moral corruption and failed loyalty and cheap cruelty around it." We cannot help but admire the dignity of the Lord Jesus Christ as he goes through this indignity. He does it with magnanimity and with the sense that he is not forsaken. He is not out of control. God's providence is ruling over all. So the character and the calmness of Jesus remind us and provide an example for us in the midst of our own trials.

Peter feebly attempts to stop the Lord Jesus Christ from being arrested. Peter had pledged to Jesus that he would be faithful to the end and that he would die with or for him if necessary. This incident seemed to be Peter's opportunity to make good on his pledge. It is, however, important to realize that Peter's actions—as brave as they are—reveal a fundamental misunderstanding of Jesus' mission and the purpose of his death.

As Jesus is being arrested, Matthew tells us that one of his disciples attempted to resist the arrest by taking out his short sword and cutting off the ear of a servant of the High Priest. Matthew—very kindly—does not tell you that this is Peter. But Peter, as he assists Mark in the writing of his Gospel, raises his hand in the corner of the room and fesses up. Peter shows by his actions that he did not understand the purpose of what Jesus was going to do in the next twenty-four hours. He is revealing to us a deficiency of understanding. Peter is not only saying, "Lord, forbid it," as he did in Matthew 16, when Jesus began preparing his disciples to understand that he had to die. He is attempting to physically prevent the Lord Jesus Christ from being arrested, persecuted, and killed.

Jesus was conscious that God's plan was being worked out and nobody, not Peter, not Judas, not the mob, nor anyone else was going to keep that plan from being fulfilled.

Before we criticize Peter, let's admire him for a minute. I do not know how many people were with Judas, but it could have been in the hundreds—part of the Roman cohort and part of the temple guard were there. Peter was hopelessly outnumbered, and yet this man is ready to take a sword in hand and go out fighting. You cannot help but admire Peter.

But again I must stress his actions were ignorant and uncomprehending. Jesus will say twice in this passage that he had to be arrested in order that the Scriptures would be fulfilled. Jesus was conscious that God's plan was being worked out and nobody, not Peter, not Judas, not the mob, nor anyone else was going to keep that plan from being fulfilled. In fact, Jesus turns to Peter, and he says, "Do you not think that I could call upon twelve legions of angels, and they would not be here like that to protect me?" Let us take Jesus literally for a moment. A Roman legion had about six thousand men in it. So if an angelic legion had six thousand angels, Jesus was saying that God could send seventy-two thousand angels in the snap of a finger to protect him. In other words, there would have been about six thousand angels for each of the eleven disciples and Jesus to protect them—not just one guardian angel, but six thousand guardian angels per individual.

In this statement, Jesus is stressing that he is not going to the cross because God lacks the power to stop it. Nor does Jesus lack the ability to ask of God to spare him. Instead, Jesus is going to the cross because he has chosen to go to the cross. He is not a passive victim. He is the prime actor and has chosen to go to the cross.

Jesus is going to the cross because he has chosen to go to the cross. Jesus goes to the cross because of his desire to fulfill the word of God. J. C. Ryle explains this beautifully, "We see in these words [*how then will the Scripture be fulfilled which says it must happen this way*] the secret of His voluntary submission to His foes. He came on purpose to fulfil the types and promises of the Old Testament Scriptures, and by fulfilling them to provide salvation for the world. He came intentionally to be the true Lamb of God, the Passover Lamb. He came to be the Scape-goat on whom the iniquities of the people were to be laid. His heart was set on accomplishing this great work. It could not be done without the 'hiding of his power' for a time. To do it he became a willing sufferer. He was taken, tried, condemned, and crucified entirely of His own free will."[2]

If you do not understand this, then you do not understand the cross. The cross is not some sort of "Plan B."

In Matthew 26:55–56, Jesus addresses his captors. The first thing he does is chide them for being cowards. Jesus says, "Why have you come under the cover of darkness? I sat in the temple in the daylight, in the open, teaching day after day. Why didn't you come then?" Jesus is pricking their consciences. They are afraid of the multitudes, and so they have come by night. Furthermore, he says, "Why do you come with swords and clubs? I have never carried a weapon. I am not a revolutionary. You utterly mistake the kind of kingdom that I'm bringing in."

Notice too that Jesus does not just acquiesce to God's sovereignty. He doesn't just shrug his shoulders and say, "Well, I guess God has allowed this terrible thing to happen." We do that sometimes, but not Jesus. Jesus said, "God has caused and decreed this to happen. This is in accordance with his holy will, which he has established before the foundation of the world. I embrace it, because it is the will of my heavenly Father, and it is good. It may be horrendous for me, but I willingly embrace it, because it is good for his people, and I love his people. He has promised to give them to me if I lay down my life for them." Jesus reveled in the sovereignty of God, and he proclaims it even to the multitude of captors.

Jesus' responses to his captors are interesting and instructive. First, he calls Judas a friend. I do not think Jesus is being sarcastic with Judas; instead, Jesus is handing out one more warning to Judas. If you have any doubts about the free offer of the gospel, look how Jesus behaved in Matthew 26 and 27. Even to Judas, he is casting out strands of mercy with the hope of pulling him in.

Second, Jesus carefully explains to his captors that he is being arrested because he is the Son of God who came into the world to seek and save those who were lost. Even during his betrayal, Jesus is an evangelistic preacher attempting to plant the seed of grace in the hearts of these men who are part of his betrayal and his arrest.

But in spite of all this, as Jesus is being led away, all his disciples flee. I suspect that 2 Timothy 2:11–13 speaks very directly to that situation. Paul says, "The saying is trustworthy, for: If we died with him, we will also live with him; if we endure, we will also reign with him; If we deny him, he also will deny us; if we are faithless, he remains faithful—for he cannot deny himself." Judas had denied Jesus and was thus denied. It is tempting for us to put the disciples in the same lump with Judas because of their desertion, but apparently Jesus' weak and well-meaning disciples were not denying him here. Instead, they were simply faithless. So Jesus loved them anyway. He was faithful, though they were faithless.

Sometimes we do not know the weakness of our heart until we are tried and tested. Have you ever gotten excited and were moved at a Christian meeting of some sort? In your zeal, you resolve to be faithful to Christ like never before. But in forty-eight hours or seventy-two hours, you found yourself falling prey to sin once again. My friends, J. C. Ryle reminds us, "Let us settle it in our minds, that there is nothing too bad for the very best of us to do unless he watches, prays, and is held up by the grace of the Lord Jesus Christ."[3] If the actions of the disciples in verse 56 teach us anything, they teach us not to trust in ourselves, but to wholly lean on Jesus' name.

Adapted from "The Hour Is at Hand: Jesus Betrayed: According to Scripture," sermon by Ligon Duncan III, First Presbyterian Church, Jackson, Mississippi, December 5, 1999. Used by permission.

Scripture quotations are from *The Holy Bible, English Standard Version®*.

7

THEN DID THEY SPIT IN HIS FACE

Charles Spurgeon

"Then they spit in his face and struck him. And some slapped him."

Matthew 26:67

Let us go in thought to the palace of Caiaphas the high priest, and there let us, in deepest sorrow, realize the meaning of these terrible words: "Then did they spit in his face." There is more of deep and awful thunder in them than in the bolt that bursts overhead, there is more of vivid terror in them than in the sharpest lightning flash: "Then did they spit in his face."

Observe that these men, the priests, and scribes, and orders, and their servitors, did this shameful deed after they had heard our Lord say, "Hereafter shall ye see the Son of man sitting on the right hand of power, and coming in the clouds of heaven" (Matt. 26:64). It was in contempt of this claim, in derision of this honor

43

which he foretold for himself, that "then did they spit in his face," as if they could bear it no longer, that he, who stood to be judged of them, should claim to be their Judge; that he, whom they had brought at dead of night from the garden of Gethsemane as their captive, should talk of coming in the clouds of heaven: "Then did they spit in his face."

Nor may I fail to add that they thus assaulted our Lord after the high priest had rent his clothes. My brethren, do not forget that the high priest was supposed to be the representative of everything that was good and venerable among the Jews. The high priest was the earthly head of their religion; he it was who, alone of mortal men, might enter within the mysterious veil; yet he it was who condemned the Lord of glory, as he rent his clothes, and said, "He hath spoken blasphemy; what further need have we of witnesses? behold, now ye have heard his blasphemy" (Matt. 26:65). It makes me tremble as I think of how eminent we may be in the service of God, and yet how awfully we may be enemies of the Christ of God. Let none of us think that, though we even clamber up to the highest places in the church, we are therefore saved. We may be high priests, and wear the Urim and the Thummim, and put on the breastplate with all its wondrous mystic stones, and bind around us the curious girdle of the ephod, and yet, for all that, we may be ringleaders in expressing contempt of God and of his Christ. It was when Caiaphas, the high priest, had pronounced the word of condemnation against Christ, that "then did they spit in his face."

There are two or three thoughts that come to my mind when I think that these wicked men did actually spit in Christ's face—in that face which is the light of heaven, the joy of angels, the bliss of saints, and the very brightness of the Father's glory. This spitting shows us, first, how far sin will go. If we want proof of the depravity of the heart of man, I will not point you to the stews of Sodom and

Gomorrah, nor will I take you to the places where blood is shed in streams by wretches like to Herod and men of that sort. No, the clearest proof that man is utterly fallen, and that the natural heart is enmity against God, is seen in the fact that they did spit in Christ's face, did falsely accuse him, and condemn him, and lead him out as a malefactor, and hang him up as a felon that he might die upon the cross. Why, what evil had he done? What was there in his whole life that should give them occasion to spit in his face? Even at that moment, did his face flash with indignation against them? Did he look with contempt upon them? Not he; for he was all gentleness and tenderness even toward these his enemies, and their hearts must have been hard and brutal indeed that "then did they spit in his face." He had healed their sick, he had fed their hungry, he had been among them a very fountain of blessing up and down Judaea and Samaria; and yet, "then did they spit in his face." Humanity stands condemned of the blackest iniquity now that it has gone as far as to spit in Christ's face.

The clearest proof that man is utterly fallen, and that the natural heart is enmity against God, is seen in the fact that they did spit in Christ's face.

O my brothers, let us hate sin; O my sisters, let us loathe sin, not only because it pierced those blessed hands and feet of our dear Redeemer, but because it dared even to spit in his face! No one can ever know all the shame the Lord of glory suffered when they did spit in his face. These words glide over my tongue all too smoothly; perhaps even I do not feel them as they ought to be felt, though I would do so if I could. But could I feel as I ought to feel in sympathy with the terrible shame of Christ, and then could I interpret those feelings by any language known to mortal man, surely you would bow your heads and blush, and you would feel rising within your spirits a burning indignation against the sin that dared to put the Christ of God to such shame as this. I want to kiss his feet when I think that they did spit in his face.

Then, once more, my thoughts run to him again in this way, I think of the tender omnipotence of his love. How could he bear this spitting when, with one glance of his eye, had he been but angry, the flame might have slain them, and withered them all up? Yet he stood still even when they did spit in his face; and they were not the only ones who thus insulted him, for, afterwards, when he was taken by the soldiers into Pilate's hall, they also spat upon him in cruel contempt and scorn.

If you prefer your merits to his, it must be said of you also, "Then did they spit in his face."

I want to bring the truth home, brethren, and to show you how we may have done to Christ what these wicked men did. "Oh!" says one, "I was not there; I did not spit in his face." Listen; perhaps you even have spat in his face.

There are still some who spit in Christ's face by denying his Godhead. They say, "He is a mere man; a good man, it is true, but only a man"; though how they dare say that, I cannot make out, for he would be no good man who claimed to be God if he was not God. Jesus of Nazareth was the basest of impostors who ever lived if he permitted his disciples to worship him, and if he left behind him a life which compels us to worship him, if he was not really and truly God; therefore, of all those who declare that he is not God—and there is a very great company of them even amongst the nominally religious people of the present day—we must sorrowfully, but truthfully say, "Then did they spit in his face."

They also do the same who rail at his gospel. There are many who seem as if they cannot be happy unless they are tearing the gospel to pieces. Especially is that divine mystery of the substitutionary sacrifice of Christ. We delight to know that our Lord Jesus Christ suffered in the room and place and stead of his people.

Yet I have read some horrible things which have been written against that blessed doctrine, and as I read them I could only say to myself, "Then did they spit in his face." If there is anything that is beyond all else the glory of Christ, it is his atoning sacrifice; and if ever you thrust your finger into the very apple of his eye, and touch his honor in the tenderest possible point, it is when you have aught to say against his offering of himself a sacrifice unto God, without blemish and without spot, that he might put away the iniquities of his people. Wherefore judge yourselves in this matter, and if ye have ever denied Christ's deity, or if ye have ever assailed his atoning sacrifice, it might truly have been said of you, "Then did they spit in his face."

Further, this evil is also done when men prefer their own righteousness to the righteousness of Christ. There are some who say, "We do not need pardon, we do not want to be justified by faith in Christ, we are good enough already," or, "We are working out our own salvation; we mean to save ourselves." O sirs, if you can save yourselves, why did Jesus bleed upon the cross? It was a superfluity indeed that the Son of God should die in human form if there be a possibility of salvation by your own merits; and if you prefer your merits to his, it must be said of you also, "Then did they spit in his face."

The same thing is, oh! so sadly true when anyone forsakes the profession of being a follower of Christ's. There are some, alas! who, for a time, have appeared to stand well in the church of God—I will not judge them—but there have been some who, after making a profession of religion, have deliberately gone back to the world. After seeming for a while to be very zealous, they have become worldly, gay, and perhaps even lascivious and vile. They break the Sabbath, they neglect the Word of God, they forsake the mercy-seat; and their last end is worse than their first. When a man forsakes Christ for a harlot, when he gives up heaven for

47

gold, when he resigns the joys he professed to have had in Christ in order that he may find mirth in the company of the ungodly, it is another instance of the truth of these words, "Then did they spit in his face." To prefer any of these things to Christ, is infamous; and the mere act of spitting from the mouth seems little compared with this sin of spitting with the very heart and soul and pouring contempt upon Christ by choosing some sin in preference to him. Yet, alas! how many are thus still spitting in Christ's face.

If ever anybody should despise us for Christ's sake, let us not count it hard, but let us be willing to bear scorn and contempt for him. Let us say to ourselves, "Then did they spit in his face. What, then, if they also spit in mine? If they do, I will 'hail reproach, and welcome shame,' since it comes upon me for his dear sake." See, that wretch is about to spit in Christ's face! Put your cheek forward, that you may catch that spittle upon your face, that it fall not upon him again, for as he was put to such terrible shame, every one who has been redeemed with his precious blood ought to count it an honor to be a partaker of the shame, if by any means we may screen him from being further despised and rejected of men.

Adapted from "An Awful Contrast," sermon (2473) by C. H. Spurgeon, intended for reading on Lord's Day, July 12, 1896, Metropolitan Tabernacle, Newington, given Lord's day evening, July 11, 1886.

Scripture quotations are from the *King James Version* of the Bible.

8

THE SILENCE OF THE LAMB
Adrian Rogers

He was oppressed, and he was afflicted,
yet he opened not his mouth;
like a lamb that is led to the slaughter,
and like a sheep that before its shearers is silent,
so he opened not his mouth.

Isaiah 53:7

"Now the chief priests and the whole Council were seeking false testimony against Jesus that they might put him to death, but they found none, though many false witnesses came forward. At last two came forward and said, 'This man said, "I am able to destroy the temple of God, and to rebuild it in three days."' And the high priest stood up and said, 'Have you no answer to make? What is it that these men testify against you?' But Jesus remained silent. . . ."

Matthew 26:59–63

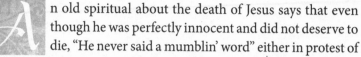

n old spiritual about the death of Jesus says that even though he was perfectly innocent and did not deserve to die, "He never said a mumblin' word" either in protest of his unfair treatment or to defend himself. We need to learn why Jesus stood before his accusers and crucifiers and "opened not his mouth" (Isa. 53:7) and what the silence of the Lamb of God means for us.

How different Jesus' response at his trials and crucifixion is from ordinary human nature. Even when we have done something wrong and know we are wrong, still the first words that tend to form in our mouths are words of excuse and self-defense.

And what about when we are right but blamed for being wrong? Most of us would be quick to speak up and protest our innocence. It's just human nature to want to speak up and justify ourselves.

But Jesus met his accusers with silence, even as the prophet Isaiah wrote seven hundred years before the fact. Isaiah 53:7 continues, "He is brought as a lamb to the slaughter, and as a sheep before her shearers is dumb, so he openeth not his mouth."

How does a lamb respond to its executioner? With meekness and submission. Here is a picture of the Lord Jesus Christ, who was and is absolutely sinless, being unjustly accused and yet offering no defense or excuse whatsoever. There was no protest from his lips as he was slandered, and he made no effort to avoid the false accusations and the cross that would follow.

Jesus never protested or sought to justify himself. He was silent in the face of his accusers.

This is true even though the trials Jesus endured—and there were about six altogether—were held illegally and were a mockery of justice. It was crass, coldhearted sin that judged Jesus guilty and brought him to the cross. The interesting thing is that Jesus never protested or sought to justify himself. He was silent in the face of his accusers. This facet of his passion and death leads to a great lesson for our lives and a great blessing for our hearts.

Over and over again the Bible records the silence of God's Lamb in the presence of his accusers. We read in Matthew 26 concerning Jesus' middle-of-the night trial at the palace of the Jewish high priest, Caiaphas: "The high priest arose, and said unto him, Answerest thou nothing? what is it which these witness against thee? But Jesus held his peace . . ." (vv. 62–63; see also Mark 14:60–61). This is amazing, especially given that the witnesses hurling charges against Jesus were giving false testimony (Matt. 26:59–61).

Now let me say that when we talk about the silence of Jesus during his passion, we are not saying that he never uttered one word at any point in any of his trials. In Matthew 26 the high priest finally said, "I adjure thee by the living God, that thou tell us whether thou be the Christ, the Son of God. Jesus saith unto him, Thou hast said . . ." (vv. 63–64).

What Caiaphas did here was to put Jesus under oath before God, and so he was obliged to answer. Jesus could not and did not deny who he is. But this was not an act of self-defense or self-justification in the face of false witnesses. It was simply the truth. So the point is still made that the Lord Jesus offered no explanation for his actions or the charges made against him.

We see a similar reaction in John 18:33 when Pilate asked Jesus during their private conversation, "Art thou the King of the Jews?" Jesus answered Pilate with a question of his own because Pilate needed to see the truth. So the Roman governor pressed on: "Art thou a king then?" Jesus answered, "Thou sayest that I am a king" (v. 37). But notice again that there is nothing in the way of excuse or defense in this exchange. The fact is that Pilate was on trial in his questioning of Jesus, and Jesus wanted Pilate to realize that fact.

When it came to those who accused and blasphemed Jesus, the Bible records: "When he was accused of the chief priests and elders, he answered nothing. Then said Pilate unto him, Hearest thou not how many things they witness against thee? And he answered him to never a word; insomuch that the governor marvelled greatly" (Matt. 27:12–14; see also Mark 15:1–5).

Let me give you one more telling example of Jesus' silence. After Pilate had finished examining Jesus and had made his decision against the truth, he compounded his sin by having the Lord scourged and beaten. But then the Jews scared Pilate by saying that Jesus deserved death because he had claimed to be the Son of God. In great fear, Pilate ran back into the judgment hall and asked Jesus, "Whence art thou?" (John 19:9). But the Bible says, "Jesus gave him no answer," because he had nothing left to say to Pilate. This pandering Roman politician had already turned a blind eye to the truth.

When we read these Scriptures, we wonder why Jesus did not say something to vindicate himself. Again, it is the natural tendency of our human flesh to justify ourselves when we are guilty—and even more so when we are innocent and are being falsely accused.

Jesus held back any words that would have relieved him from the shame and blame of sin.

Why was the dear Savior so silent? I believe we find at least part of the answer in the great prophecy of Isaiah 53: "Surely he hath borne our griefs, and carried our sorrows: yet we did esteem him stricken, smitten of God and afflicted. But he was wounded for our transgressions, he was bruised for our iniquities: the chastisement of our peace was upon him; and with his stripes we are healed. All we like sheep have gone astray; we have turned every one to his own way; and the LORD hath laid on him the iniquity of us all" (vv. 4–6).

Going on to verse 10, we read: "Yet it pleased the LORD to bruise him; he hath put him to grief: when thou shalt make his soul an offering for sin, he shall see his seed, he shall prolong his days, and the pleasure of the LORD shall prosper in his hand." The apostle Paul put it this way: "For he hath made him to be sin for us, who knew no sin; that we might be made the righteousness of God in him" (2 Cor. 5:21).

The Bible teaches us that when Jesus Christ took our sin, he took all of the punishment that goes with that sin. A part of that punishment is shame. Had Jesus defended himself and protested his innocence, he would have suffered no shame, and that would have left us guilty.

Jesus could not prove himself innocent and then die in our place the shameful death that we deserve. Thank God that Jesus was willing to be counted a sinner before God, that we might be counted as righteous before God!

Jesus held back any words that would have relieved him from the shame and blame of sin. He was not a sinner, but he took fully the sinner's place.

And here's another thought to consider. If Jesus had risen up in his own defense during his trials, I believe that he would have been so powerful and irrefutable in making his defense that no governor, high priest, or other legal authority on earth could have stood against him!

In other words, if Jesus had taken up his own defense with the intention of refuting his accusers and proving his innocence, he would have won! But we would have lost, and we would be lost for all eternity.

They accused Jesus of blasphemy, lying, sedition, and many other things, but the Savior answered not a word. This is the amazing silence of the Lamb.

Excerpted from *The Passion of Christ and the Purpose of Life* by Adrian Rogers. Copyright © 2005 by Adrian Rogers. Used by permission of Crossway Books.

Scripture quotations are from the *King James Version* of the Bible.

9

The Sufferings of Christ

J. C. Ryle

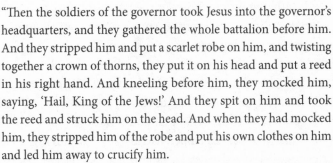

"Then the soldiers of the governor took Jesus into the governor's headquarters, and they gathered the whole battalion before him. And they stripped him and put a scarlet robe on him, and twisting together a crown of thorns, they put it on his head and put a reed in his right hand. And kneeling before him, they mocked him, saying, 'Hail, King of the Jews!' And they spit on him and took the reed and struck him on the head. And when they had mocked him, they stripped him of the robe and put his own clothes on him and led him away to crucify him.

As they went out, they found a man of Cyrene, Simon by name. They compelled this man to carry his cross. And when they came to a place called Golgotha (which means Place of a Skull), they offered him wine to drink, mixed with gall, but when he tasted it, he would not drink it. And when they had crucified him, they divided his garments among them by casting lots. Then they sat down and kept watch over him there. And over his head they put the charge against him, which read, 'This is Jesus, the King of the Jews.' Then two robbers were crucified with him, one on the right and one on the left. And those who passed by derided him, wagging their heads and saying, 'You who would destroy the temple and rebuild it in three days, save yourself! If you are the Son of God, come down from the cross.' So also the chief priests, with the scribes and elders, mocked him, saying, 'He saved others; he cannot save himself. He is the King of Israel; let him come down now from the cross, and we will believe in him. He trusts in God; let God deliver him now, if he desires him. For he said, "I am the Son of God."' And the robbers who were crucified with him also reviled him in the same way."

Matthew 27:27–44

The catalog of all the pains endured by our Lord's body is indeed a fearful one: seldom has such suffering been inflicted on one body in the last few hours of life. The most savage tribes, in their refinement of cruelty, could hardly have heaped more agonizing tortures on an enemy than were heaped on the flesh and bones of our beloved Master. Never let it be forgotten that he had a real human body, a body exactly like our own, just as sensitive, just as vulnerable, just as capable of feeling intense pain. And then let us see what that body endured.

Our Lord, we must remember, had already passed a night without sleep, and endured excessive fatigue. He had been taken from Gethsemane to the Sanhedrin, and from the Sanhedrin to Pilate's judgment hall. He had been put on trial twice and unjustly condemned twice. He had already been flogged and beaten cruelly with sticks. And now, after all this suffering, he was handed over to the Roman soldiers, a body of men no doubt expert in cruelty, and of all the people, least likely to behave with delicacy or compassion. These hard men at once proceeded to work their will. They "gathered the whole company of soldiers round him" (v. 27); they stripped our Lord and put on him, in mockery, a scarlet robe (v. 28); they "twisted together a crown of thorns" (v. 29); they spat on him and "struck him on the head again and again" (v. 30); and finally, having put his clothes on him, they led him out of the city to a place called Golgotha (v. 33), and there crucified him between two thieves.

But what was a crucifixion? Let us try to realize it and understand its misery. The person crucified was laid on his back on a piece of timber, with a cross-piece nailed to it near one end—or on the trunk of a tree with branching arms, which answered the same purpose: his hands were spread out on the cross-piece, and nails driven through each of them, fastening them to the wood; his feet in like manner were nailed to the upright part of the cross. Then, the body having been securely fastened, the cross was raised up and fixed firmly in the ground. And there hung the unhappy sufferer, till pain and exhaustion brought him to his end—not dying suddenly, for no vital part of him was injured; but enduring the most excruciating agony from his hands and feet, and unable to move.

Such was the death on the cross. Such was the death Jesus died for us! For six long hours he hung there before a gazing crowd, naked, and bleeding from head to foot—his head pierced with thorns, his back lacerated with flogging, *In his death, no less than in his life, he was perfect.* his hands and feet torn with nails, and mocked and reviled by his cruel enemies to the very last.

Let us meditate frequently on these things: let us often read over the story of Christ's cross and passion. Let us remember, not least, that all these horrible sufferings were borne without a murmur; no word of impatience crossed our Lord's lips. In his death, no less than in his life, he was perfect. To the very last, Satan had no hold on him (John 14:30).

All our Lord Jesus Christ's sufferings were vicarious. He suffered not for his own sins, but for ours. He was eminently our substitute in all his passion.

This is a truth of the deepest importance. Without it the story of our Lord's sufferings, with all its minute details, must always seem mysterious and inexplicable. It is a truth, however, of which the Scriptures speak frequently. We are told that Christ "bore our sins in his body on the tree" (1 Pet. 2:24); that he "died for sins once for all, the righteous for the unrighteous" (1 Pet. 3:18); that "God made him who had no sin to be sin for us, so that in him we might become the righteousness of God" (2 Cor. 5:21); that he became "a curse for us" (Gal. 3:13); that "Christ was sacrificed once to take away the sins of many people" (Heb. 9:28); that "he was pierced for our transgressions, he was crushed for our iniqui-ties" (Isa. 53:5); and that "the LORD has laid on him the iniquity of us all" (Isa. 53:6). May we all remember these texts. They are among the foundation-stones of the gospel.

Our sins twisted the crown of thorns; our sins drove the nails into his hands and feet; on account of our sins his blood was shed. Surely the thought of Christ crucified should make us loathe all sin.

But we must not be content with a vague general belief that Christ's sufferings on the cross were vicarious. We are intended to see this truth in every part of his passion. We may follow him all through, from the bar of Pilate to the minute of his death, and see him at every step as our mighty substitute, our represen-tative, our head, our surety, our proxy—the divine friend who undertook to stand in our place and, by the priceless merit of his suffer-ings, to purchase our redemption. Was he flogged? It was done so that "by his wounds we are healed" (Isa. 53:5). Was he condemned, though innocent? It was done so that we might be acquitted, though guilty. Did he wear a crown of thorns? It was done so that we might wear the crown of glory. Was he stripped of his clothes? It was done so that we might be clothed in everlasting righteousness. Was he mocked and reviled? It was done so that we might be honored and blessed. Was he reckoned a criminal, and counted among those who have done wrong? It was done so that we might be reckoned innocent, and declared free from all sin. Was he declared unable to save himself? It was so that he might be able to save others to the uttermost. Did he die at last, and that the most painful and disgraceful death? It was done so that we might live forevermore, and be exalted to the highest glory.

Let us ponder these things well: they are worth remembering. The very key to peace is a right apprehension of the vicarious sufferings of Christ.

And let us learn from the story of the passion always to hate sin with a great hatred. Sin was the cause of all our Savior's sufferings. Our sins twisted the crown of thorns; our sins drove the nails into his hands and feet; on account of our sins his blood was shed. Surely the thought of Christ crucified should make us loathe all sin. As the Church of England Homily of Passion says so well: "Let this image of Christ crucified be always printed in our hearts. Let it stir us up to the hatred of sin, and provoke our minds to the earnest love of Almighty God."

Excerpted from *Matthew (Expository Thoughts on the Gospels)* by J. C. Ryle. Copyright © 1993 by Watermark. Used by permission of Crossway Books.

Scripture references are from *The Holy Bible: New International Version*®.

$\mathfrak{F}$ATHER, $\mathfrak{F}$ORGIVE $\mathfrak{T}$HEM

John MacArthur

"And Jesus said, 'Father, forgive them, for they know not what they do. . . .'"

Luke 23:34

"He poured out his soul to death
and was numbered with the transgressors;
yet he bore the sin of many,
and makes intercession for the transgressors."

Isaiah 53:12

 ne of the significant factors about the crucifixion narratives in all four Gospels is the silence of Christ before his accusers. When Christ *did* speak in those final hours before he gave up his life, it was clear that his mind was not on revenge—not even on self-defense. *Forgiveness* was the predominant theme of his thoughts throughout the whole ordeal of his crucifixion.

For example, at the height of his agony, at the very moment when most victims of crucifixion might scream out in fury with a curse, he prayed for forgiveness for his tormentors: "Father, forgive them; for they do not know what they are doing . . ." (Luke 23:34).

Jesus was praying that when they came to grips with the enormity of what they had done and sought God's forgiveness for it, he would not hold it against them.

Bishop J. C. Ryle wrote, "These words were probably spoken while our Lord was being nailed to the cross, or as soon as the cross was reared up on end. It is worthy of remark that as soon as the blood of the Great Sacrifice began to flow, the Great High Priest began to intercede."[1]

Do you see the glory of that? Although Christ is the sovereign, eternal, omnipotent God, he did not threaten, he did not condemn, he did not pronounce doom on his crucifiers. Instead of lashing out against them, he prayed for them.

Jesus had earlier taught, "Love your enemies and pray for those who persecute you" (Matt. 5:44). But who would have thought that teaching would be carried to such an extreme?

Like so many aspects of our Lord's death, this manifestation of divine mercy was a fulfillment of Old Testament prophecy. Isaiah 53:12 foretold it: "He poured out Himself to death, and was numbered with the transgressors; yet He Himself bore the sin of many, *and interceded for the transgressors.*"

This was the reason for which he had come (John 3:17). The whole point of the incarnation was forgiveness. It was the very thing Jesus was dying for. It was what he was praying for. And it is what he exemplified in his death. Again, he gave us an example we are solemnly charged to follow. If you don't feel somewhat inadequate to answer that calling, perhaps you have not understood the full significance of it.

Inevitably someone will ask whom Christ was praying for. Was it the Jews who had conspired to sentence him to death? The Roman soldiers who actually nailed him to the cross, then gambled for his clothing? The mocking crowd who taunted him?

The answer must be all of the above, and more. In one sense the scope of the prayer surely extends beyond the people who were there that day to every person who has ever trusted Christ and so received his forgiveness. After all, our sins put him there. We are every bit as culpable as the men who actually drove those nails through his sinless hands and feet.

Now, "Father, forgive them" was not a prayer for immediate, unconditional, indiscriminate forgiveness of everyone who participated in Christ's crucifixion. Rather, it was a plea on behalf of those who would repent and trust him as their Lord and Savior. Jesus was praying that when they came to grips with the enormity of what they had done and sought God's forgiveness for it, he would not hold it against them. Forgiveness does not belong to those who stubbornly persist in unbroken unbelief and sin and rebellion. Those who carried their steely hatred of him to the grave were not absolved from their crime by this prayer.

Forgiveness is offered to all, freely (Rev. 22:17). God is as eager to forgive as the prodigal's father was. He pleads for every sinner to turn to him in humble repentance (Ezek. 18:3–32; Acts 17:30). Those who do, he promises to receive with open arms and unrestrained forgiveness. But those who remain in infidelity and defiance will never know God's forgiveness.

So Christ was praying for those who would repent of their evil deed. The sin they were guilty of was so unbelievably horrific that if these people had not actually heard him pray for their forgiveness, they might have assumed their sin was unforgivable.

Why did he pray, "*Father*, forgive them," when in the past he had simply forgiven sinners himself (cf. Luke 7:48)? After all, hadn't he already shown that "the Son of Man has authority on earth to forgive sins" (Matt. 9:6)?

Yes, but now as our sin-bearer, he was taking our place, dying in our stead, having surrendered every divine prerogative, including his own life, on our behalf. He hung there before God as a representative of sinful humanity. And so he appealed to *the Father* to forgive the transgressors. He was as that moment identifying himself with the very ones whose irrational hatred of him had brought him all these sorrows. Such is the wonder of divine mercy!

Jesus' words, "For they do not know what they are doing" (Luke 23:34), obviously do not mean that those who killed him were wholly ignorant of the awful reality of their crime. The Jewish leaders knew that they had falsely accused him (Matt. 26:59). Pilate knew that Jesus was an innocent man (Luke 23:4). Anyone even slightly aware of what was going on would have seen that a great injustice was being done (Mark 14:56).

Yet these were blind people led by blind rulers (Acts 3:17). They were all utterly ignorant of the magnitude of their atrocity. They were completely blind to the spiritual light of divine truth.

Their ignorance, however, did not excuse them. Ample evidence testified to the truth of who Jesus was. The people had heard him teach, and they "were amazed as His teaching; for He was teaching them as one having authority, and not as their scribes" (Matt. 7:28–29). They had witnessed his mighty works (John 10:32–33). In all probability, some of those now clamoring for his death were the same people who earlier had followed him just for his miracles' sake. Some of them may have even been among the multitudes he fed (John 6:26). Perhaps many of them had been part of the throng who just a week earlier had hailed him as he entered the city (Matt. 21:8–11)! Surely these people could not have been ignorant of the things Jesus had said and done in their presence. Two things are certain: their ignorance itself was not excusable, and ignorance certainly did not excuse their crime of murder.

Yet our Lord in his great mercy prayed for their forgiveness. Spiritually, they were blind, utterly insensitive to the awful reality of what they had done. It was not as if they consciously and deliberately were trying to snuff out the Light of the world. Their own minds were utterly blind to that true Light, and therefore they could not have understood the full enormity of their crime. "If they had understood it, they would have not crucified the Lord of glory" (1 Cor. 2:8).

The forgiveness he extended on the cross to those who put him to death is the same forgiveness he extends to sinners today.

In a sense, every pardoned sinner who ever lived is an answer to Christ's prayer. Since our guilt put him on the cross in the first place, we bear responsibility for his death just as surely as those who actually drove the nails through his hands and feet. And the forgiveness he extended on the cross to those who put him to death is the same forgiveness he extends to sinners today. We who have experienced such forgiveness have a solemn duty to extend a similar mercy to others as well (Eph. 4:32).

What a high standard he set for us! His refusal to retaliate, his silent acceptance of others' wrongs against him, his prayer of forgiveness, his eagerness to forgive—all set an example we are expected to follow.

How quickly our flesh recoils from following that example! When we suffer wrongfully, it becomes very easy to rationalize a counterattack and painfully difficult to follow our Lord's steps. But like him, we must keep entrusting ourselves to the One who "judges righteously" (1 Pet. 2:23).

Can we look at this scene in the cross and understand the depth of his passion, then justify our own unwillingness to forgive any offense our neighbor might have committed against us? The answer is obvious. Should we not extend mercy even as we have received mercy (cf. Matt. 18:21–35)? As those who have been forgiven much, we owe much, both to our Lord and to our fellow servants (cf. Luke 7:47). May the Lord grant us grace to follow in his steps of mercy!

Excerpted from *The Freedom and Power of Forgiveness* by John F. MacArthur. Copyright © 1998 by John F. MacArthur. Used by permission of Crossway Books.

Scripture references are from *The New American Standard Bible*®.

11

ᴡITH ᴌOUD ᴄRIES AND ᴛEARS

John Owen

"In the days of his flesh, Jesus offered up prayers and supplications, with loud cries and tears, to him who was able to save him from death, and he was heard because of his reverence. Although he was a son, he learned obedience through what he suffered."

Hebrews 5:7–8

"And about the ninth hour Jesus cried out with a loud voice. . . ."

Matthew 27:46

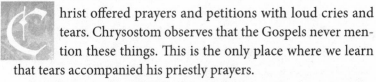hrist offered prayers and petitions with loud cries and tears. Chrysostom observes that the Gospels never mention these things. This is the only place where we learn that tears accompanied his priestly prayers.

In prophecy the prayers that are meant here are called his "groaning": "Why are you so far from saving me, so far from the words of my groaning?" (Ps. 22:1). This "roaring" or "groaning" is a strong and vehement outcry. Psalm 32:3 says, "When I kept silent, my bones wasted away through my groaning all day long." The vehemency of his complaints consumed his natural strength. So Job 3:24, "For sighing comes to me instead of food; my groans pour out like water." A sense of extreme pressure and distress is signified in the words, "I am feeble and utterly crushed; I groan in anguish of heart." This is, again, a strong cry. Psalm 22:9–21 has in nearly every sentence a spirit of roaring, groaning, or a strong cry. It is not just the outward noise, but the inner heart and soul this is principally intended.

It is the same with the evangelists in the Gospels. The prayers offered with loud cries and tears are those prayed to God during his passion, both in the garden and on the cross. Luke 22:44 declares, "And being in anguish, he prayed more earnestly, and his sweat was like drops of blood falling to the ground." This inner frame of mind here reflects what our apostle is referring to when he mentions loud cries and tears. Christ was totally possessed by an "agony" or "anguish," that is, a strong and vehement conflict of mind, in and about the dreadful and terrible things, which has been called "a dread of utter ruin" by the commentator Nemes, and "a dread of evil to come upon us from outside" by Aquinas. Jesus prayed "more earnestly" with more vehement anguish of mind, spirit, and body. For the word denotes the highest degree of earnestness that the mind, spirit, and body are capable of. This produced that preternatural sweat, "like drops of blood," falling off him onto the ground. About this he says in Psalm 22:14, "I am poured out like water. . . ."

The Lord Christ learned obedience when he experienced it in practice.

Again, on the cross itself, it is said, "Jesus cried out in a loud voice . . ." (Matt. 27:46). This is how Christ prayed his priestly prayers that related to his offering himself as a sacrifice, which the evangelists record.

The object of Christ's offering is described as the one who could save him from death and had the power to do this. God is intended here. The apostle does not call him God, or the Father of Christ, even though the Lord Jesus, in these prayers, calls upon him, using both of these names. So, in the garden, Christ calls him Father: "My Father, if it is possible, may this cup be taken from me . . ." (Matt. 26:39). On the cross Christ called him God: "My God, my God, why have you forsaken me?" (Matt. 27:46). Christ calls him Father again as he places his life and soul into his hands: "Father, into your hands I commit my spirit . . ." (Luke 23:46). But our apostle does not use these expressions in Hebrews 5, and only describes God as the one who could save him from death. He does this to show the Lord Christ's thoughts about God at this time as he faced death and reflected on its consequences. His purpose is to declare what frame of mind Christ was in during his suffering and offering of himself.

And he was heard because of his reverent submission. To be heard in Scripture means two things. First, it signifies to be accepted, even if the request is denied. "God will hear me" is equivalent to "God will accept me, and is pleased with my supplications" (see Ps. 55:17). Second, to be heard means to have our request answered. To be heard is to be delivered. It is expressed like this in Psalm 22:24: "For he has not despised or disdained the suffering of the afflicted one; he has not hidden his face from him but has listened to his cry for help." In the first sense there is no doubt that the Father always heard the Son. As John 11:42 states, "I knew that you always hear me. . . ." Always, in all things, God the Father accepted the Lord Christ and was well pleased with him. But we ask here how far the Lord Christ was heard in the latter way. Was he so heard as to be delivered from what he prayed against?

Christ's prayers fall into two categories with regard to this: conditional and absolute. As far as his conditional prayers were concerned, Luke 22:42 is a prime example: "Father, if you are willing, take this cup from me; yet not my will, but yours be done." Christ would not have been human if he had not experienced extreme aversion to things that were about to happen to him. This expression of his nature, in his mind and will and emotions, which were completely holy in him, our Savior expressed in that conditional prayer. This prayer was answered in the following ways. His mind was strengthened against the terror of the impending events. This enabled him to be perfectly composed to embrace God's will: "not my will, but yours be done." So Christ was heard to the extent he had wished to be heard. Although, by nature, he desired deliverance, since he was human, yet he did not desire this absolutely, as he was wholly given over to God's will.

The main prayers he offered up to him who was able to save him from death were absolute, and in them he was absolutely heard and delivered. He hoped, trusted, and believed in God's deliverance, and therefore prayed absolutely for it. "Because the Sovereign LORD helps me, I will not be disgraced. Therefore have I set my face like flint, and I know I will not be put to shame. He who vindicates me is near. Who then will bring charges against me? . . ." (Isa. 50:7–8). Here he was heard absolutely.

Reverent submission. The word for reverent comes in only one other place in the New Testament: Hebrews 12:28, "let us be thankful, and so worship God acceptably with reverence and awe." However, in its adjectival form it comes three times—in Luke 2:25, Acts 2:5, and Acts 8:2—where it is translated "devout," and "God-fearing," and "godly." In Hebrews 11:7 the verb derived from this word is translated as "holy fear." Christ's soul was engaged in a conflict in the sense that his faith and trust in God were tried to the limit by the attacks of fear about what would happen to him during his passion. In all this Christ showed his reverent submission to God's will.

Although he was a son, he learned obedience from what he suffered. It was not unknown for a son or child adopted by God to be disciplined, to suffer, and to learn to be obedient. But we are not talking about a son or child of God here; we are talking about the Son of God, God's own Son (see John 1:14; Rom. 8:3; Phil. 2:6). That the Son of God should go through the things spoken about here is indeed a wonder. Therefore it is said of him, although he was a son. . . .

Three questions may be asked of this verse: first, what is the obedience referred to here? Second, how did Christ "learn" obedience? And third, by what means did Christ learn obedience?

The word "obedience" means to be obedient to someone else's command. The word has come to mean to "hear" or to "listen to." Hence, to "listen" or "hear" is often used in Scripture to mean "obey." To disobey is to "refuse to listen." In Christ, this obedience may be said to be general and particular.

Christ's obedience is said to be general in that his whole life in this world was in line with God's will. This obedience to God was the life and beauty of Christ's holiness. Christ was obedient in particular events. He "became obedient to death—even death on a cross!" (Phil. 2:8). His Father had commanded him to lay down his life, and Christ did this in an obedient manner. Far from being rebellious, he offered his back to those who beat him and his cheeks to those who pulled out his beard (see Isa. 50:5–6).

Christ is said to have learned obedience. This kind of "learning" is what a humble disciple does as he receives instruction. Here it says about the Lord Christ that he learned obedience, not that he learned to obey. This sheds light on the whole subject. It is possible to talk about learning obedience in three senses. Fist, we can learn obedience through coming to know what our duty is. The psalmist says, "Before I was afflicted I went astray . . ." (Ps. 119:67). In this way the psalmist was taught what duties God required of him. But our Lord Jesus did not learn obedience in this sense, nor could he do so. For he knew beforehand all he would have to go through. God's law was in his heart, and he never forgot God or his law.

It is possible to speak of "learning obedience" in the sense that one is instructed, guided, helped, and directed. In this way we "learn" obedience as we are gradually instructed in the knowledge and practice of it. But the Lord Christ did not learn obedience in this sense. He had fullness of grace always with him and in him, directing him and guiding him. Being full of grace, truth, and wisdom, he was never at a loss about what to do.

It is, however, possible to say that the Lord Christ learned obedience when he experienced it in practice. In the sense that a person knows the taste of meat by eating it, it may be said of our Savior that he "tasted death" when he experienced death. One special kind of obedience is intended here, namely, a submission to great, hard, and terrible things, accompanied by patience and quiet endurance and faith for deliverance from them. This Christ could have not experience of, except by suffering the things he had to pass through, exercising God's grace in them all. Thus, Christ learned obedience.

The way or means by which Christ learned obedience is stated: from the things that he suffered. And we cannot exclude from here anything Christ suffered throughout his life on earth. But since the apostle is especially concerned with Christ as high priest, what he suffered refers to his death and the events leading up to his death. He "became obedient to death—even death on a cross!" (Phil. 2:8). Through his sufferings Christ learned obedience as he had occasion to exercise the graces of humility, meekness, patience, and faith. While these graces always lived with him, they were not capable of being exercised in this special way except through his sufferings.

Adapted from *Hebrews* by John Owen. Copyright © 1998 by Watermark. The Crossway Classic Commentaries, edited by Alister McGrath and J. I. Packer. Used by permission of Crossway Books.

Scripture references are from *The Holy Bible: New International Version*®.

12

Ҭhat Ꮊe Ꮇight Ꭰestroy the Ꮃorks of the Ꭰevil

Martyn Lloyd-Jones

> "Since therefore the children share in flesh and blood, he himself like-wise partook of the same things, that through death he might destroy the one who has the power of death, that is, the devil, and deliver all those who through fear of death were subject to lifelong slavery."
>
> Hebrews 2:14–15

ave you ever been filled with a sense of amazement and wonder at the drama of the cross? Have you ever looked at it in these terms—the drama, the conflict, the fight? How did our Lord ever come to such a place, what brought him there? Ah, you say, that was men who did not understand him. Is that a sufficient and an adequate answer? My dear friend, can you not see the devil behind men? What was the office of Jesus of Nazareth? To whom did he do any harm? What was wrong with his teaching? What was wrong with his miracles? What was wrong with his acts of kindness? He came to do good, he came to teach, he came to deliver mankind. What reception did he get? Well, look at it in the Pharisees and scribes, look at their bitterness and hatred, look at their scorn and their derision, look at their blasphemy. Look at it not only there, but also in the Roman governor, Pilate. Look at it in King Herod, the King of the Jews, look at it in the common people. Can you not see this terrible blasphemy, this scorn? Why all this feeling, why all this hatred, why all this vituperation? There is only one explanation. It is the devil that is fighting. It is the devil in these men and women.

This is the devil's great blunder, that by bringing the Son of God to the cross he was defeating himself and bringing about his own ultimate doom.

You see it running right through the records in the four Gospels. Read the account of what happened to him: "And when they had plaited a crown of thorns, they put it upon his head, and a reed in his right hand: and they bowed the knee before him, and mocked him, saying, Hail, King of the Jews! And they spit upon him, and took the reed, and smote him on the head. And after they had mocked him, they took the robe off from him, and put his own raiment on him, and led him away to crucify him" (Matt. 27:29–31). Or again, "And they that passed by"—when he is actually nailed to the tree—"reviled him, wagging their heads and saying, Thou that destroyest the temple, and buildest it in three days, save thyself. If thou be the Son of God, come down from the cross. Likewise also the chief priests mocking him, with the scribes and elders, said, He saved others; himself he cannot save. If he be the King of Israel, let him now come down from the cross, and we will believe him. He trusted in God; let him deliver him now, if he will have him: for he said, I am the Son of God. The thieves also, which were crucified with him, cast the same in his teeth" (vv. 39–44).

Here is an innocent man. Nobody can bring any evidence against him. He has done no wrong. Indeed he has done nothing but good in the world. He came to help people and to teach, but look at the spite, look at the mocking and the spitting and the jeering and the scoffing. What is the matter with them? There is only one answer to the question—he gave it himself. He said, "But this is your hour, and the power of darkness" (Luke 22:53); these people do not know what they are doing. That is why he prayed on the cross and said, "Father, forgive them; for they know not what they do . . ." (Luke 23:34). And indeed they did not know what they were doing.

The world was very pleased with itself, was it not, as it looked upon him there dying upon the cross? That is why they laugh. That is why they are joking. At last they had got him, they had nailed him, they had killed him. He was finished.

Was he? "Having spoiled principalities and powers, he made a shew of them openly, triumphing over them in it" (Col. 2:15). And yet here they are, they think they have reached the hour of victory, they have got this one whom they hate, and the devil was delighted. If only he could kill him, that would be the end. And that was his terrible miscalculation. He did not realize, and this is the devil's great blunder, that by bringing the Son of God to the cross he was defeating himself and bringing about his own ultimate doom. How? Well, the apostle tells us that our Lord there on the cross, in apparent weakness, was putting the devil and his powers to an open shame and that he was triumphing over them.

And the Lord does it in this way. The power of the devil is, after all, nothing but a usurped power. He has no power of his own. The devil is the god of this world, the prince of the power of the air, for one reason only, and that is that man in sin has gone out of the kingdom of God, and therefore is in the kingdom of the devil. The devil has no power over man, except that man is estranged from God and is no longer in touch with the power of God. The only one who can master the devil is God. And the moment we are out of touch with God, we are mastered by the devil, and we are his helpless tools, and victims in his kingdom like goods in a palace. And that is the position of the entire human race.

There is only one power that can deliver a man out of the clutches of hell and of the devil. It is the power of God. But how can I have that power? I have sinned against God; I am a rebel against him.

The devil thought he was defeating Christ, but Christ was reconciling us to God, defeating the devil and delivering us out of his clutches.

God's wrath is upon me. Before I can know the power of God I must be reconciled to God. And that was the very thing that was happening on the cross on Calvary's hill. There on the cross our Lord was reconciling us unto God. "God was in Christ, reconciling the world unto himself, not imputing their trespasses unto them . . ." (2 Cor. 5:19). We are reconciled to God, and the power of God takes over and delivers us from the devil and his cohorts and transfers us into the kingdom of God. That is why the apostle puts it like this in Colossians 1:13: "Who hath delivered us from the power of darkness, and hath translated us into the kingdom of his dear Son." That is how it happens. That is what was happening upon the cross. The devil thought he was defeating Christ, but Christ was reconciling us to God, defeating the devil and delivering us out of his clutches.

Here is one of the most wonderful things about the cross. Here is one of the most glorious reasons for glorying in the cross. Here Christ defeated our ultimate enemy, the devil, the one who originally brought man and the universe down. He was cast out, he was defeated. He has been put in chains. And finally, he is going to be completely and utterly destroyed. He will be cast into the lake of fire with the beasts and all the false prophets. And he will have no more power.

Excerpted from *The Cross* by Martyn Lloyd-Jones. Copyright © 1986 by Bethan Lloyd-Jones. used by permission of Crossway Books.

Scripture quotations are from the *King James Version* of the Bible.

13

I Am Thirsty

Joseph "Skip" Ryan

"After this, Jesus, knowing that all was now finished, said (to fulfill the Scripture), 'I thirst.'"

John 19:28

Jesus was dying. He was terribly thirsty. The hot, arid, Middle Eastern sun was beating down upon him. People in the ancient Middle East knew something about death by dehydration that we may not know. In the first stages of dehydration, one feels an inward caving in or longing. But then as the thirst goes on, it actually becomes a deep and profound burning inside. Our bodies are 98 percent water. When they do not have water to replenish what they themselves are, every molecule begins to cry out. Spiritually speaking, if God is not at the center of our souls, then we do not have that which can ultimately meet our thirst and quench it. The real danger of that thirst is eternal death in hell.

C. S. Lewis gives us a wonderful way to understand hell when he says, "Heaven is the place where man says to God, 'Thy will be done,' and hell is that place where God says to man, 'Thy will be done.'"[1] Hell is the place where we get more and more of what we have been seeking to quench our thirst. Hell is the place where we get more than we ever wanted of those things that we are trying to stuff into our souls.

When he says, "I am thirsty," he is saying, "I am thirsty with a thirst that every sinner deserves to experience forever."

Jesus tells the remarkable little parable in Luke 16 about a poor man, Lazarus, who is the servant of a wealthy man. Both of them die within a short period of time; Lazarus goes to heaven, and the rich man goes to hell. From hell the rich man prays to Father Abraham, who is in heaven with Lazarus, "Father Abraham, would you send Lazarus down to dip his finger and give me just a little taste of water, because it is so hot down here?" (see Luke 16:24).

It is interesting that there is no sign of repentance in what the rich man says. In fact, he is still giving Lazarus orders as if he were still his servant. "Fetch me water," he says (see v. 24). There is no sign that he understands that the things he has been seeking to fill his soul will not satisfy him at all.

When Jesus says, "I am thirsty," I don't think he means physical thirst, because in the whole passion account we never once hear Jesus complaining about any of the physical torture and agony into which he is placed. He is blindfolded and beaten with the fists of soldiers. He is scourged with a whip made with bits of metal and glass fragments tied into straps that are laid repeatedly across his back. There is a crown of thorns meanly pressed into his brow until he bleeds. Never once does he complain. Never once does he say, "It hurts." So when he says, "I am thirsty," he is saying, "I am thirsty with a thirst that every sinner deserves to experience forever." He means that he is going to hell, that he is now like the rich man in hell, with no one to bring him water.

In speaking of his thirst, perhaps Jesus is thinking of Psalm 22:

> I am poured out like water,
>> And all my bones are out of joint.
>> My heart is like wax;
>> it is melted within me.
> My strength is dried up like a potsherd,
>> And my tongue cleaves to my jaws;
>> And Thou dost lay me in the dust of death. (vv. 14–15)

Jesus understands his thirst biblically. In fact, the larger context of Jesus' remark about his thirst reads, "in order that the Scripture would be fulfilled, [Jesus] said, 'I am thirsty.'" Psalm 22 begins this way: "My God, my God why hast Thou forsaken me?" (v. 1; quoted in Matt. 27:46; Mark 15:34). This thirst is primarily physical but comes about because the Son of God has now been put into hell, a hell that he does not deserve. You and I deserve that unquenchable, unremitting, agonizing thirst because we have sought to fill our lives with anything and everything but him.

At the cross, Jesus asks the question, what do you thirst after?

At the cross, Jesus asks the question, what do you thirst after? Throughout Scripture, thirst is a metaphor for a deep, inward spiritual emptiness and need. Without God we will die, because the Bible says that what we most thirst for and need at the center of our lives is not stuff but God. The question always is, what do I drink to fill that deep and profound thirst within me?

Those of us who grew up on the ocean know that sometimes you get thirsty while sailing or boating. If you run out of water, the last thing you want to do is put your mouth down into the salt water. It will only increase your thirst and accelerate the process of dehydration. Every one of us puts our mouth down into the salt water of whatever we use to meet our deepest needs. Jesus Christ became for you the One who thirsted unto death. He descended into hell, as the Apostles' Creed says. It was as if he was placed into the position of eternal separation from God that you and I deserve.

Look to Jesus and say, "You are the only One who can satisfy my deepest need. I know, Lord, even this day I will find yet more ways to stick my mouth into the salt water of this world. Nevertheless, Lord, forgive me. And nevertheless, Lord, I come to you as one who believes that You took my place and thirsted for me and descended into hell for me so that I might have life evermore." If you say this in faith, then you are at one with him, despite the fact that your sins are many.

Excerpted from *That You May Believe: New Life in the Son* by Joseph "Skip" Ryan. Copyright © 2003 by Joseph R. Ryan. Used by permission of Crossway Books.

Scripture quotations are from *The New American Standard Bible*®.

14

GOD-FORSAKEN
Philip Graham Ryken

"And about the ninth hour Jesus cried out with a loud voice, saying, 'Eli, Eli, lema sabachthani?' that is, 'My God, my God, why have you forsaken me?'"

Matthew 27:46

t was typical for crucified persons to utter loud cries from their crosses. One scholar writes that what made crucifixions especially gruesome were "the screams of rage and pain, the wild curses and the outbreaks of nameless despair of the unhappy victims."[1] Jesus' cry was not that kind of cry. It was not a cry of rage. It was not a wild curse. It was not an outbreak of nameless despair.

Jesus' cry was not that kind of cry because he did not lose hope altogether. This was the only time he spoke to his Father as "God" rather than "Father." Yet even in his agony, Jesus was still praying. He was still speaking to his Father in personal terms: "*My* God, *my* God." And after all, Jesus' loud cry was only a question, though it arose out of his personal experience of alienation and abandonment. It was the cry of a man who felt forsaken by God, a man who was entering the abyss of death and was about to be swallowed up by darkness.

The question Jesus cried out on the cross was first asked by King David a millennium before Jesus lived. It comes from the overture to Psalm 22: "My God, my God, why have you forsaken me? Why are you so far from saving me, so far from the words of my groaning? O my God, I cry out by day, but you do not answer, by night, and am not silent" (Ps. 22:1–2). The Son of God reiterated that question from the cross.

Jesus did not just feel forsaken, he was forsaken.

There is no answer. God did not deliver Jesus from the cross. The only answers he received were silence and darkness, the silence of being forsaken by God and the darkness of God's judgment descending upon the earth.

Jesus did not just *feel* forsaken, he *was* forsaken. It was not just that Jesus experienced passing sensations of alienation and rejection on the cross. It was more than that. The question Jesus shouted out from the cross pointed back to an actual experience, to an objective state of affairs, to something that had already happened to him: "Why *have you forsaken* me?" Jesus Christ could tell when his intimacy with God the Father was interrupted. When that happened, he knew that he had been forsaken.

Why did it happen? Why did God the Father forsake God the Son on the cross? We cannot comprehend it. We cannot explain it. The great theologian Martin Luther said, "God forsaken by God, who can understand that?" If even Jesus himself could not fully understand it, then we cannot understand it either.

But we can at least say this: it had something to do with what Jesus was doing on the cross. What Jesus was doing on the cross was bearing sin, carrying sin, wearing sin. Jesus was taking the sins of the world upon his shoulders. It was as if God had taken a giant bucket and scooped up all the sins of his people—all the jealousy and the anger and the lying, all the rebellion and the stealing and the incest, all the hypocrisy and the envy and the swearing—and dumped them all out on Jesus Christ. "The LORD has laid on him the iniquity of us all" (Isa. 53:6). "God made him who had no sin to be sin for us . . ." (2 Cor. 5:21).

Once he had done that, God the Father had to forsake all that sin. When Jesus was wearing our sin on the cross, God the Father could not bear to look at the sin or at his Son. He had to avert his gaze. He had to shield his eyes. He had to turn his back. He had to condemn and reject and curse and damn that sin. When he carried our sin, Christ became "a curse for us, for it is written: 'Cursed is everyone who is hung on a tree'" (Gal. 3:13). When Jesus Christ picked up our sins, he became a curse for us, and when he became a curse for us, he was accursed by God. God was not forsaking his Son as much as he was forsaking the sin the Son was carrying.

When Jesus was wearing our sin on the cross, God the Father could not bear to look at the sin or at his Son. He had to avert his gaze. He had to shield his eyes. He had to turn his back. He had to condemn and reject and curse and damn that sin.

If you want to know what God really thinks about sin and what he intends to do about it, look at Jesus rejected on the cross and listen to Jesus forsaken on the cross. That is what sin deserves: the wrath and curse of God. That is what sinners deserve: to be put to death and damned for their sins. That strikes fear into the hearts of those of us who are sinners. At least it ought to. If God was willing to forsake his own Son for the sins of others, should he not also forsake you for your sins?

The forsaking of the Son of God on the cross is a fearful thing, but it is good news for sinners who repent. It is good news because it means that when you meet Jesus Christ at the cross you are meeting someone who has experienced the full measure of the tragedy of human existence. Out of his own experience of physical suffering and spiritual rejection Jesus not only sympathizes with your pain, he empathizes with it.

The forsaking of the Son of God on the cross is also good news because it means that God's children will never be forsaken. Jesus was God-forsaken so that you might not be forsaken.

There is a strong hope in the fact that Jesus himself was not completely abandoned by his Father. Yes, he did cry out to God from the cross. Yes, he did experience separation and alienation from God as a result of our sin. Yes, he was even forsaken at the cross. But he was not forsaken forever. Jesus spoke to his Father one more time from the cross. He prayed, "Father, into your hands I commit my spirit" (Luke 23:46). The bond of fellowship between Father and Son was reestablished. The Son spoke, and the Father answered. God the Father received the spirit of Jesus when he died. He did not let Jesus rot in the grave, but he raised him back to life on the third day. Although the Son was forsaken for our sins, he was not forsaken forever.

Neither will you be forsaken. God will forsake sinners, but he will not forsake you if you will come and meet Jesus Christ at the cross. God will not forsake you if you accept Christ's sacrifice for your sins, taking your sins and placing them on Jesus' shoulders.

Jesus promises all who come to him that they will never be God-forsaken. He said what he said on the cross ("My God, my God, why have you forsaken me?") so that no son or daughter of his would ever have to utter those words of desolation again. Listen to what Jesus says now to everyone who follows him. It is a promise that even if you feel homeless in this world, you will always have a home with God:

Do not let your hearts be troubled. . . . In my Father's house are many [mansions]. . . . I am going to prepare a place for you. And if I go and prepare a place for you, I will come back and take you to be with me that you also may be where I am. . . . I will not leave you as orphans; I will come to you. (John 14:1–3, 18)

Excerpted from *The Heart of the Cross* by Philip Graham Ryken. Copyright © 1999 by James Montgomery Boice and Phillip Graham Ryken. Used by permission of Crossway Books.

Scripture references are from *The Holy Bible: New International Version*®.

15

CURSED

R. C. Sproul

"His body shall not remain all night on the tree, but you shall bury him the same day, for a hanged man is cursed by God. . . ."

Deuteronomy 21:23

"Christ redeemed us from the curse of the law by becoming a curse for us—for it is written, 'Cursed is everyone who is hanged on a tree'—"

Galatians 3:13

 od called Abraham to be a blessing for the whole world. It is as though God said, "I am going to spread out this blessedness from the center, and I'm going to let it pour out and over all the nations of the world. All nations will be blessed through you, so that all who have faith are blessed along with you."

In contrast to this blessedness that comes by faith, Paul says that all who rely on observing the Law as a means of salvation, all who trust in their own good works and their own performance, are under a curse. For it is written, "Cursed is everyone who does not continue to do everything written in the book of the law." Paul was thinking back to Deuteronomy. He was remembering the terms of the covenant. Any person who failed to keep every one of these laws was under the curse. Then Paul says clearly that no one is justified before God by the Law, "for the just shall live by faith." The Law is not based on faith. The object of saving faith is Christ because he and he alone is able to remove the curse from us:

> Christ has redeemed us from the curse of the law, having become a curse for us (for it is written, "Cursed is everyone who hangs on a tree"). (Gal. 3:13)

Paul says that in the cross Christ became a curse for us. He took upon himself all the negative sanctions of the penalties of the Law. In taking this curse he even fulfilled the cryptic statement, "cursed is everyone who hangs upon a tree."

When we look at the intricacy of the drama of the events of Jesus' crucifixion, we see that some amazing things have taken place. The Old Testament prophetic utterances are fulfilled to the most minute detail. In the first instance the Bible says that the Messiah will be delivered to the Gentiles for judgment. It happened in the course of history that Jesus was put on trial during a time of Roman occupation. Though the Romans allowed a certain amount of home rule to their conquered vassals, they did not permit the death penalty to be imposed by local rulers. The Jews did not have the authority to put Christ to death. All that they could do was to meet in council and deliver Jesus to Pontius Pilate, who acted with Roman authority. Jesus was thus delivered from his own people to the Gentiles. He was delivered "outside the camp." He was given into the hands of the pagans, outside the camp where the face of God does not shine, where the light of God's countenance does not fall. Jesus was delivered into their hands for judgment. The Jews did not kill or execute by crucifixion. They executed by stoning. But the Romans executed by crucifixion. So the method of Jesus' death was "hanging upon a tree." The Old Testament curse, remember, was not upon everyone who was stoned; it was upon "everyone who hangs upon a tree."

Then we note the site of the actual execution. It was outside of Jerusalem. It was in Jerusalem that Jesus was first delivered to the Gentiles for judgment. Once he was judged and condemned to be executed, he was forcibly led by the way of the Via Dolorosa outside the walls of the city to Golgotha. Just as the scapegoat was driven outside the camp, outside of the Holy City where the presence of God was concentrated, so Jesus was sent into the outer darkness.

Just as the scapegoat was driven outside the camp, outside of the Holy City where the presence of God was concentrated, so Jesus was sent into the outer darkness.

During the hours Jesus hung on the cross, an astronomical phenomenon occurred. In the middle of the afternoon it became dark. Darkness descended upon the land. In the midst of the intensity of this darkness, which may have involved a blotting out or obscuring of the sun (perhaps even a total eclipse), Jesus cried out. He screamed in agony, "My God, My God, why have You forsaken Me?" (Matt. 27:46). There have been various interpretations of these words of Christ. Albert Schweitzer concluded from this text that Jesus died in disillusionment. He expected that God would deliver him, but in his final moments Jesus realized that God was not coming to his rescue. So he died much as does a disillusioned, tragic Shakespearean hero. Others point out that those words are quoted from Psalm 22. They argue that Jesus was simply identifying himself with the suffering servant of Psalm 22. They say he was reciting poetry at his death. I do not doubt that the source of his word was that psalm, and that Jesus was aware of it. I'm sure he had read that psalm many times. But I think more was involved than his identification with the psalm.

My ordination hymn was "'Tis midnight, and on Olive's Brow." I love that hymn in spite of a line in it that bothers me. It declares that Jesus was "not forsaken by his God." Some theologians say, "Jesus, in his humanity, felt forsaken on the cross, but he wasn't really forsaken." But if Jesus was not really forsaken on the cross, we are still in our sins. We have no redemption. We have no salvation. The whole point of the cross is that if Jesus was going to bear our sins and the sanctions of the covenant, then he had to experience utter and complete forsakenness by the Father.

The sign of the old covenant was circumcision. In one sense it was a primitive and obscene sign. Why did the Jew cut off the foreskin of the flesh? This rite had two meanings—a positive and a negative meaning—representing the two sanctions of the covenant.

The cross represented the supreme act of circumcision. When Jesus took the curse upon himself, he so identified with our sin that he became a curse. God cut him off and justly so.

The positive meaning of cutting the foreskin was that God was cutting out this group of people from the rest, separating them, setting them apart to be a holy nation, to be a blessing. The negative was that the Jew was saying, "Oh, God, if I fail to keep every one of the terms of this covenant, may I be cut off from you, cut off from your presence, cut off from the light of your countenance, cut off from your blessedness just as I have ritually cut off the foreskin of my flesh."

As a reflection of this sign, the cross represented the supreme act of circumcision. When Jesus took the curse upon himself, he so identified with our sin that he became a curse. God cut him off and justly so. This was an act of divine justice. At the moment that Christ took

94

upon himself the sin of the world, he became the most grotesque, most obscene mass of sin in the history of the world. God is too holy to even look at iniquity. When Christ was hanging on the cross, the Father, as it were, turned his back on Christ. He removed his face. He turned out the lights. He cut off his Son. There was Jesus, who in human nature had been in a perfect, blessed relationship with God throughout his life. There was Jesus, the Son in whom the Father was well pleased. Now he hung in darkness, isolated from the Father, cut off from fellowship—fully receiving in himself the curse of God—not for his own sin but for the sin he willingly bore by imputation for our sake.

I have heard many sermons about the physical pain of death by crucifixion. I've heard graphic descriptions of the nails and the thorns. Surely the physical agony of crucifixion was a ghastly thing. But there were thousands who died on crosses and may have had more painful deaths than that of Christ. But only one person has ever received the full measure of the curse of God while on a cross. I doubt that Jesus was even aware of the nails and the spear—he was so overwhelmed by the outer darkness. On the cross Jesus was in the reality of hell. He was totally bereft of the grace and the presence of God, utterly separated from all blessedness of the Father. He became a curse for us so that we someday will be able to see the face of God. So that the light of his countenance might fall upon us, God turned his back on his Son. No wonder Christ screamed. He screamed from the depth of his soul. How long did he have to endure it? We don't know, but a second of it would have been of infinite value.

Finally, Jesus cried, "It is finished!" (John 19:30). It was over. What was over? His life? The pain of nails? No. It was the forsakenness that ended. The curse was finished.

Excerpted from *Saved from What?* by R. C. Sproul. Copyright © 2002 by R. C. Sproul. Used by permission of Crossway Books.

Scripture references are from *The New King James Version.*

16

Into Your Hands I Commit My Spirit

James Montgomery Boice

"Then Jesus, calling out with a loud voice, said, 'Father, into your hands I commit my spirit!' And having said this he breathed his last."

Luke 23:46

rom very early in the history of the church, preachers have noted that Jesus' last words show that he was in total control of the situation, as he had been in every moment of his life. For these are not the words of an exhausted man, as if Jesus merely died from dehydration, loss of blood, shock, extreme fatigue, or suffocation. Not at all. They record a deliberate act of dismissing his spirit.

Luke makes this clear by recording that Jesus said these words "with a loud voice," not as a final dying gasp. John says that Jesus "bowed his head and gave up his spirit"—that is, willingly (John

19:30). Matthew combines the two ideas, writing, "When Jesus had cried out again in a loud voice, he gave up his spirit" (27:50).

Jesus was in control all through his life, and it is the same at the very end. In the last moment of his life, Jesus simply dismissed his spirit into the hands of God. "Father, into your hands I commit my spirit."

None of us can die this way. It is possible for us to commit suicide, using some external means to snuff out our life. But we cannot simply dismiss our spirits as Jesus did.

As Jesus died, he commended his spirit to God. So may we die in like faith.

In these last words of Jesus from the cross we find that whatever we may have understood from the Lord's cry of desolation—"My God, my God, why have you forsaken me?"—whatever may have happened, this much at least is true: God had never ceased to be Jesus' Father. It was as Jesus' Father that God sent his Son into the world to die, and it is as Jesus' Father that God was waiting at the end to receive him back joyously into heaven.

We learn from Jesus' final words from the cross that there is a life beyond the grave. We know this because of the way he spoke about his spirit. He did not speak of it as if it were mere breath that he would breathe out for the last time and then die, though "spirit" (*pneuma*) does mean "breath." That is the way animals die, but it is not like that for men and women who are made in God's image and are intended for eternal life with him. Nor did he infer the death of his spirit, as if he were passing into nothingness.

As Jesus died, he commended his spirit to God. So may we die in like faith. We can echo Jesus' word knowing that as we pass from this life trusting Jesus' death on our behalf, we pass into the loving hands of the Father who is waiting in heaven to receive us to himself.

This is how the saints of all ages have died, many with these very words on their lips. These were the dying words of Stephen, the first Christian martyr. "And as they were stoning Stephen, he called out, 'Lord Jesus, receive my spirit'" (Acts 7:59, ESV). It was the same with Polycarp, the bishop of Smyrna who was martyred in AD 156 at the age of eighty-six; Martin Luther, the great Protestant reformer; Philipp Melanchthon, Luther's steady coworker and friend; Jerome of Prague; John Hus, who was burned at the stake for his faith a century before the Reformation; and an almost endless list of saints.

Jesus was filling his mind and strengthening his spirit not by trying to keep a stiff upper lip or look for a silver lining, as we might say, but by an act of deliberately remembering and consciously clinging to the great prophecies and promises of God. If Jesus did that, don't you think you should do it too?

When Hus was condemned by the Council of Constance in 1415, the bishop who conducted the ceremony ended with the chilling words, "And now we commit thy soul to the devil."

Hus calmly replied, "I commit my spirit into thy hands, Lord Jesus Christ; unto thee I commend my spirit, which thou hast redeemed."

Have you noticed that when Jesus said, "Father, into your hands I commit my spirit," he was quoting Scripture, just as we do when we say the same words? The words come from Psalm 31, which says, "Into your hands I commit my spirit; redeem me, O LORD, the God of truth" (v. 5).

This shows what Jesus was doing on the cross, particularly in these last moments. He was reflecting on Scripture. And not only on Psalm 31! "My God, my God, why have you forsaken me?" comes from Psalm 22:1. In my opinion, the words "it is finished" come from the end of the same psalm, since the words "he has done it" (v. 31) can be equally well translated, "it is finished." Even the words "I am thirsty" were spoken, according

to John who records them, so that Psalm 69:21 might be fulfilled (see John 19:28). That verse says, "They put gall in my food and gave me vinegar for my thirst."

Four of the seven last words were from the Old Testament. Only Jesus' direct addresses to God on behalf of the soldiers, to the dying thief, and to his mother and the beloved disciple were not. This means that Jesus was filling his mind and strengthening his spirit not by trying to keep a stiff upper lip or look for a silver lining, as we might say, but by an act of deliberately remembering and consciously clinging to the great prophecies and promises of God. If Jesus did that, don't you think you should do it too? And not only when you come to die.

You need to fill your head with Scripture and think of your life in terms of the promises of Scripture now. If you do not do it now, how will you ever find strength to do it when you come to die? You must live by Scripture, committing your spirit into the hands of God day by day if you are to yield your spirit into God's loving hands trustingly at the last.

17

BLOOD AND WATER

John Calvin

"But when they came to Jesus and saw that he was already dead, they did not break his legs. But one of the soldiers pierced his side with a spear, and at once there came out blood and water. He who saw it has borne witness—his testimony is true, and he knows that he is telling the truth—that you also may believe. For these things took place that the Scripture might be fulfilled: 'Not one of his bones will be broken.' And again another Scripture says, 'They will look on him whom they have pierced.'"

John 19:33–37

he fact that they broke the legs of the two robbers and then found that Christ was already dead, and therefore did not touch his body, is an extraordinary work of God's providence. Ungodly men will doubtless say that it happens naturally that one man die sooner than another. But if we examine carefully the whole narrative, we shall be forced to ascribe this to God's hidden purpose, that Christ's death happened much more quickly than people expected, so there was no need to break his legs.

One of the soldiers pierced Jesus' side with a spear. The soldier pierced Christ's side with his spear to find out if he was dead; but God had a higher purpose in mind. Some people have deceived themselves by imagining that the "sudden flow of blood and water" was a miracle. It is natural that the blood, when it is congealed, should lose its red color and resemble water. It is well known also that water is contained in the membrane which immediately adjoins the intestines.

Christ came "by water and blood" (1 John 5:6). By these words he means that Christ brought the true atonement and the true washing.

The evangelist takes great pains to explain that blood flowed with the water, as if he were relating something unusual and different to nature.

But his intention was quite different. He wanted to fit his narrative in with the passages of Scripture which he immediately adds, and more especially with what believers might infer from it when he says elsewhere that Christ came "by water and blood" (1 John 5:6). By these words he means that Christ brought true atonement and the true washing. Forgiveness of sins and justification, as well as the sanctification of the soul, were prefigured in the law by those two symbols of sacrifices and ablutions for appeasing God's wrath. Ablutions were the tokens of true holiness, remedies for purging uncleanness and removing the stains of the flesh.

That faith may no longer rest on these factors, John declares that the fulfillment of both of these graces is in Christ; and here he gives us a visible token of the same fact. The sacraments which Christ left with his church have the same purpose: the purification and sanctification of the soul, which consists of "a new life" (Rom. 6:4) and which is highlighted in our baptism and which is in the Lord's Supper the pledge of a perfect atonement.

But these are very different from the ancient figures of the law, for they show Christ as present, whereas the figures of the law pointed to him as still absent and at a distance. For this reason I do not object to what Augustine says, that our sacraments have flowed from Christ's side; for when baptism and the Lord's Supper lead us to Christ's side to draw from it, as from a well which they represent, then we are truly washed from our pollutions and are renewed to a holy life and live before God, redeemed from death and delivered from condemnation.

He is wounded by the sins of his people, and especially by their obstinate contempt of his Word, just as a mortal man receives a deadly wound when his heart is pierced.

"Not one of his bones will be broken." This quotation is taken from Exodus 12:46 and Numbers 9:12, where Moses refers to the paschal lamb. John takes it for granted that that lamb was a figure of the true and only sacrifice through which the church was to be redeemed. This is consistent with the fact that it was sacrificed as the memorial of a redemption which had been already made. As God intended it to celebrate the former favor, he also intended that it should show the spiritual deliverance of the church, which was still in the future. So Paul without any hesitation applies to Christ the rule which Moses lays down about eating the lamb: "For Christ, our Passover lamb, has been sacrificed. Therefore let us keep the Festival, not with the old yeast, the yeast of malice and wickedness, but with bread without yeast, the bread of sincerity and truth" (1 Cor. 5:7–8).

From this analogy, or similarity, faith derives great benefit, since in all the ceremonies of the law it views the salvation which has been displayed in Christ. This is the purpose of the evangelist John when he says that Christ was not only the pledge of our redemption but also its price in that we see accomplished in him what was formerly seen by the ancient people under the figure of the

Passover. In this way the Jews are also reminded that they ought to seek in Christ the substance of everything that the law prefigured but did not actually accomplish.

"They will look on the one they have pierced." This passage is violently distorted by those who try to interpret it literally as referring to Christ. This is not the evangelist's purpose in quoting it. Rather, he shows that Christ is that God who had complained, through Zechariah, that the Jews had pierced his heart (Zech. 12:10). God speaks there in a human way, declaring that he is wounded by the sins of his people, and especially by their obstinate contempt of his Word, just as a mortal man receives a deadly wound when his heart is pierced. He says elsewhere that his spirit was deeply grieved (see Matt. 26:38).

Now, as Christ is God and "appeared in a body" (1 Tim. 3:16), John says that in his visible body was clearly fulfilled what his divine majesty had suffered from the Jews, so far as it was capable of suffering. Not that God is at all affected by the outrages of men or that the reproaches which are thrown at him from the earth ever reach him, but by this expression he wanted to declare the great sacrilege which the wickedness of men is guilty of when it rebels against heaven. What was done through the hand of a Roman soldier the evangelist John justly imputes to the Jews; thus they are elsewhere accused, "whom you crucified, both Lord and Christ" (Acts 2:36), even though they did not lay a finger on his body.

Excerpted from *John* by John Calvin. Copyright © 1994 by Watermark. The Crossway Classic Commentaries, edited by Alister McGrath and J. I. Packer. Used by permission of Crossway Books.

Scripture references are from *The Holy Bible: New International Version*®.

18

฿E ᗞESCENDED INTO ฿ELL
AND ᴀSCENDED INTO ฿EAVEN

J. I. Packer

He descended into hell;
the third day he rose again from the dead;
he ascended into heaven. . . .
　　　　　　—from the Apostle's Creed

eath has been called "the new obscenity," the nasty thing that no polite person nowadays will talk about in public. But death, even when unmentionable, remains inescapable. The one sure fact of life is that one day, with or without warning, quietly or painfully, it is going to stop. How will I, then, cope with death when my turn comes?

Christians hold that the Jesus of the Scriptures is alive, and that those who know him as Savior, Lord, and Friend find in this knowledge a way through all life's problems, dying included. For "Christ leads me through no darker rooms than he went through before." Having tasted death himself, he can support us while we taste it, and carry us through the great change to share the life beyond death into which he himself has passed. Death without Christ is "the king of terrors," but death with Christ loses the "sting," the power to hurt, which it otherwise would have.

John Preston, the Puritan, knew this. When he lay dying, they asked him if he feared death, now it was so close. "No," whispered Preston; "I shall change my *place*, but I shall not change my *company*." As if to say: I shall leave my friends, but not my Friend, for he will never leave me.

This is victory—victory over death, and the fear it brings. And it is to point the way to this victory that the Apostle's Creed, before announcing Jesus' resurrection, declares: "he descended into hell." Though this clause did not establish itself in the Creed till the fourth century, and is therefore not used by some churches, what it says is of great importance, as we can now see.

The English is misleading, for "hell" has changed its sense since the English form of the Creed was fixed. Originally, "hell" meant the place of the departed as such, corresponding to the Greek *Hades* and the Hebrew *Sheol*. That is what it means here, where the Creed echoes Peter's statement that Psalm 16:10, "thou wilt not abandon my soul to Hades" (so RSV: AV has "hell"), was a prophecy fulfilled when Jesus rose (see Acts 2:27–31). But since the seventeenth century, "hell" has been used to signify only the state of final retribution for the godless, for which the New Testament name is *Gehenna*.

What the Creed means, however, is that Jesus entered, not *Gehenna*, but *Hades*—that is, that he really died, and that it was from a genuine death, not a simulated one, that he rose.

Perhaps it should be said (though one shrinks from laboring something so obvious) that "descended" does not *imply* that the way from Palestine to Hades is down into the ground, any more than "rose" implies that Jesus returned to surface level up the equivalent of a mine shaft! The language of descent is used because Hades, being the place of the disembodied, is *lower* in worth and dignity than is life on earth, where body and soul are together and humanity is in that sense whole.

"Being put to death in the flesh but made alive in the spirit" (1 Pet. 3:18), Jesus entered Hades, and Scripture tells us briefly what he did there.

We can face death knowing that when it comes we shall not find ourselves alone. He has been there before us, and he will see us through.

First, by his presence he made Hades into Paradise (a place of pleasure) for the penitent thief (cf. Luke 23:43), and presumably for all others who die trusting him during his earthly ministry, just as he does now for the faithful departed (see Phil. 1:21–23; 2 Cor. 5:6–8).

Second, he perfected the spirits of Old Testament believers (Heb. 12:23; cf. 11:40), bringing them out of the gloom which Sheol, the "pit," had hitherto been for them (cf. Ps. 88:3–6, 10–12), into this same Paradise experience. This is the core of truth in Medieval fantasies of the "harrowing of hell."

Third, 1 Peter 3:19 tells us that he "made proclamation" (presumably, of his kingdom and appointment as the world's judge) to the imprisoned "spirits" who had rebelled in antediluvian times (presumably, the fallen angels of 2 Peter 2:4ff., who are also the "sons of God" of Genesis 6:1–4).

What makes Jesus' entry into Hades important for us is not, however, any of this, but simply the fact that now we can face death knowing that when it comes we shall not find ourselves alone. He has been there before us, and he will see us through.

Suppose that Jesus, having died on the cross, had stayed dead. Suppose that, like Socrates or Confucius, he was now no more than a beautiful memory. Would it matter? We should still have his example and teaching; wouldn't they be enough?

Had Jesus not risen, but stayed dead, the bottom would drop out of Christianity, for four things would then be true.

First, to quote Paul, 1 Corinthians 15:17: "If Christ has not been raised, your faith is futile and you are still in your sins."

Second, there is then no hope of our rising either; we must expect to stay dead, too.

Third, if Jesus Christ is not risen, then he is not reigning and will not return, and every single item in the Creed after "suffered and was buried" will have to be struck out.

Fourth, Christianity cannot be what the first Christians thought it was—fellowship with a living Lord who is identical with the Jesus of the Gospels. The Jesus of the Gospels can still be your hero, but he cannot be your Savior.

To show that it views Jesus' resurrection as fact of history, the Creed actually times it—"the third day," counting inclusively (the ancients' way) from the day when Jesus was "crucified under Pontius Pilate" in about AD 30. On that precise day, in Jerusalem, capital of Palestine, Jesus came alive and vacated a rock tomb, and death was conquered for all time.

Can we be sure it happened? The evidence is solid. The tomb was empty and nobody could produce the body. For more than a month after, the disciples kept meeting Jesus alive, always unexpectedly, usually in groups (from two to five hundred). Hallucinations don't happen this way!

The disciples, for their part, were sure that the risen Christ was no fancy, and tirelessly proclaimed his rising in face of ridicule, persecution, and even death—a most effective way of scotching the malicious rumor that they stole Jesus' body (cf. Matt. 28:11–15).

The corporate experience of the Christian church over nineteen centuries chimes in with the belief that Jesus rose, for the risen Lord truly "walks with me and talks with me along life's narrow way," and communion with him belongs to the basic Christian awareness of reality.

No sense can be made of any of this evidence save by supposing that Jesus really rose.

What is the significance of Jesus' rising? In a word, it marked Jesus out as Son of God (Rom. 1:4); it vindicated his righteousness (John 16:10); it demonstrated victory over death (Acts 2:24); it guaranteed the believer's forgiveness and justification (1 Cor. 15:17; Rom. 4:25) and his own future resurrection, too (1 Cor. 15:18); and it brings him into the reality of resurrection life now (Rom. 6:4). Marvelous! You could speak of Jesus' rising as the most hopeful—hope-full—thing that has ever happened, and you would be right!

"He ascended" echoes Jesus' "I ascend" (John 20:17). "Into heaven" echoes "taken up from you into heaven," the angels' words in the ascension story (Acts 1:10). But what is "heaven"? Is it the sky, or outer space? Does the Creed mean that Jesus was the first astronaut? No, both it and the Bible are making a different point.

"Heaven" in the Bible means three things: (1) The endless, self-sustaining life of God. In this sense, God always dwelt "in heaven," even when there was no earth. (2) The state of angels or men as they share the life of God, whether in foretaste now or in fullness hereafter. In this sense, the Christian's reward, treasure, and inheritance are all "in heaven" and heaven is shorthand for the Christian's final hope. (3) The sky, which being above us and more like infinity than anything else we know, is an emblem in space and time of God's eternal life, just as the rainbow is an emblem of his everlasting covenant (see Gen. 9:8–17).

Bible and Creed proclaim that in the ascension, forty days after his rising, Jesus entered heaven in sense 2—in a new and momentous way: thenceforth he "sitteth on the right hand of God the Father almighty," ruling all things in his Father's name and with his Father's almightiness for the long-term good of his people. "On the right hand of God" signifies not a palatial location but a regal function: see Acts 2:33ff.; Romans 8:34; Ephesians 1:20ff.; Hebrews 1:3, 13; 10:12ff.; 12:2. He "ascended far above the heavens" (that is, reentered his pre-incarnate life, a life unrestricted by anything created) "that he might fill all things" (that is, make his kingly power effective everywhere; see Eph. 4:10). "Ascended" is, of course, a picture-word implying exaltation ("going up!") to a condition of supreme dignity and power.

"Ascended" is, of course, a picture-word implying exaltation ("going up!") to a condition of supreme dignity and power.

What happened at the ascension, then, was not that Jesus became a spaceman, but that his disciples were shown a sign, just as at the transfiguration. As C. S. Lewis put it, "they saw first a short vertical movement and then a vague luminosity (that is what 'cloud' presumably means . . .) and then nothing."[1] In other words, Jesus' final withdrawal from human sight, to rule till he returns to judgment, was presented to the disciples' outward eye as a going up into heaven in sense 3. This should not puzzle us. Withdrawal had to take place somehow, and going up, down, or sideways, failing to appear or suddenly vanishing were the only possible ways. Which would signify most clearly that Jesus would henceforth be reigning in glory? That answers itself. So the message of the ascension story is: Jesus the Savior reigns!

Excerpted from *Growing in Christ* by J. I. Packer. Copyright © 1994 by J. I. Packer. Used by permission of Crossway Books.

Scripture references are from *The Revised Standard Version*.

19

A Sweet-Smelling Savor to God

Jonathan Edwards

"Christ loved us and gave himself up for us, a fragrant offering and sacrifice to God."

Ephesians 5:2

"He has appeared once for all at the end of the ages to put away sin by the sacrifice of himself."

Hebrews 9:26

hrist's death was a sacrifice to satisfy divine justice for our sins. But Christ did not merely pay a debt by his death but merited infinitely by it. He did not only satisfy God for what he as our surety owed him but also brought God infinitely into debt to him.

'Tis commonly said that Christ satisfied justice by his suffering and merited by his righteousness. But then this is to be understood

111

thus—that Christ by his sufferings considered enduring the punishment of the law without any consideration of the holiness and excellency of the act of submitting to those sufferings. Christ's death thus may be distinguished from his righteousness, but consider it as it was—a holy act of obedience, an expression of love and respect to God and his glory, an act infinitely lovely in the eyes of the Father. So it was not only an expiation for sin but a part, and the principle part, of his righteousness by which he merited.

When we consider Christ's death only as an expiation for sin, we have no consideration at all of the excellency of the act but only its equivalency to the punishment that we had deserved. But if we consider that holiness and loveliness of it in the sight of God as his voluntary act, so it doth not merely expiate our guilt but merits an infinitely glorious reward.

God was well pleased with his Son. He was not only well pleased with our surety so far that his anger was appeased, but so that he infinitely delighted in him for his righteousness' sake.

'Tis thus especially that the sacrifice Christ offered is said to be a sweet-smelling savor to God. 'Tis as there was a righteousness in it. It was as Christ in offering up this sacrifice offered up to God a heart full of divine and holy love and respect to God's authority and command. He expresses such a love by his voluntary bearing or going through those sufferings.

This made Christ's sacrifice not only satisfactory to appease his anger, but it was a sweet-smelling savor to merit his favor. Ephesians 5:2 says, "Christ also hath loved us, and hath given himself for us an offering and a sacrifice to God for a sweetsmelling savor." By this especially it was that God was well pleased with his Son. He was not only well pleased with our surety so far that his anger was appeased, but so that he infinitely delighted in him for his righteousness' sake. Isaiah 42:21 says, "The LORD is well pleased for his righteousness. . . ."

If Christ by his being slain merited for himself his own exaltation, then doubtless he has thereby merited glorious things for us. For it was for ourselves that he was slain. It was upon our account that he laid down his life. And if that act of Christ was so excellent and meritorious as to merit such a glorious reward as being exalted at God's right hand, doubtless there is merit enough for us. The happiness is exceedingly glorious that we shall have as the fruit of it, if we are in Christ. If there was merit enough in Christ laying down his life to purchase that immense glory, doubtless there is enough in that and in his other righteousness to purchase for us as much as we can desire and as much as we can enjoy.

Though Christ be fully rewarded, yet there is merit for us because believers have the benefit of Christ's merits as being in Christ and so partaking with him. Though Christ is fully rewarded in himself for his own merits, yet that doesn't argue but that those who are in him as members of him should partake in the merit and that as such they should have a right to the reward though they have no separate right to what Christ has merited.

This is part of the reward that he sought and merited—that believers should be glorified with him. This he greatly set his heart on and earnestly sought this. It was the joy that was set before him. And this he now greatly rejoices in. Herein consists the success of his undertaking, Christ has merited success. Herein he triumphs over Satan. Herein consists much of the glory of his kingdom of grace in bringing home souls to God and to eternal glory. This removes all the difficulty of the objections against Christ's meriting anything for us in that he has as much glory himself in his own exaltation as he merited. For part of that glory consists in this—that believers should be glorified.

Adapted from "Christ Was Worthy of His Exaltation upon the Account of His Being Slain" by Jonathan Edwards, in *The Glory and Honor of God: Volume 2 of the Previously Unpublished Sermons of Jonathan Edwards,* edited by Michael D. McMullen. Copyright © 2004 by Michael McMullen. Used by permission of Broadman & Holman.

Scripture quotations are from the *King James Version* of the Bible.

20

THE MOST IMPORTANT WORD IN THE UNIVERSE

Raymond C. Ortlund Jr.

"For all have sinned and fall short of the glory of God, and are justified by his grace as a gift, through the redemption that is in Christ Jesus, whom God put forward as a propitiation by his blood, to be received by faith. . . ."

Romans 3:23–25

The English language has about eight hundred thousand words. Most of us get by with around two thousand words. That means that about 788,000 words are sitting on the shelves, just waiting to be dusted off and used. The top ten most frequently used English words "are," "the," "of," "and," "to," "a," "in," "that," "is," "I," and "it"—but not "propitiation." When was the last time you heard that word? When was the last time you used it? We don't hear it on the radio or television, because we've lost the vocabulary of God. But it's the most important word in the universe. We need to recover not only the Word of God but the words of God. His words define relevance.

The word "propitiation" comes from the Latin *propitio*, meaning "to render favorable, to appease, to conciliate." To propitiate God means to appease his anger. Propitiation is all about God's wrath.

God's wrath? Wait a minute. Is God a fuming, frustrated person? Does he have a temper? Is he subject to mood swings? Is biblical propitiation like the pagan concept of throwing a virgin into the volcano to placate the pineapple god? And what if God changes back to anger? After all, we keep sinning—in the same old ways, too.

The first thing to say is that the wrath of God is a part of the gospel. It's the part we tend to ignore. Yet we don't mind our own anger. There is a lot of anger in us, a lot of righteous indignation. Listen to talk radio. In our culture it's acceptable to vent our moral fervor at one another. We watch it on cable TV news every night. It's our entertainment. But the thought of *God* being angry—well, who does he think he is?

Great question. Who *is* God? He's the most balanced personality imaginable. He is normal. His wrath is not *God's anger* an irrational outburst. God's wrath is *worthy* *shows how serious* *of God*. It is his morally appropriate, carefully *his love is.* considered, justly intense reaction to our evil demeaning his worth and destroying our own capacity to enjoy him. God cares about that. He is not a passive observer. He's involved emotionally.

The Bible says, "God is love" (1 John 4:8, 16). It never says, "God is anger." But it couldn't say that God is love without his anger, because God's anger shows how serious his love is.

What we must understand is that God's wrath is *perfect*, no less perfect than "the riches of his kindness and forbearance and patience" (Rom. 2:4). His wrath is the solemn determination of a doctor cutting away the cancer that's killing his patient. And this Doctor hates the cancer. He will rid his universe of it all. He has scheduled a "day of wrath when God's righteous judgment will be revealed" (Rom. 2:5).

God presented Christ Jesus as a propitiation by his blood (see Rom. 3:24–35). Do you see the beauty in that? In human religions, it's the worshiper who placates the offended deity with rituals and sacrifices and bribes. But in the gospel, it's God himself who provides the offering. At the cross of Christ, God put something forward. He declared something to the whole world. He presented, he displayed, the clearest statement about himself he has ever made. What was he saying? Two things.

One, he detests our evil with all the intensity of the divine personality. If you want to know what your sin deserves from God, don't look within yourself, don't look at your own emotions. Look at that man on the cross— tormented, gasping, bleeding. Take a long, thoughtful look. God was presenting something to you there. God was saying something about his perfect emotions toward your sin. He was displaying his wrath.

The God you have offended doesn't demand your blood; he gives his own in Christ Jesus.

Two—here is the other thing God was presenting at the cross— the God you have offended doesn't demand your blood; he gives his own in Christ Jesus. He knows what you deserve, but he wants to give you what you don't deserve. He himself has opened the way. He took the initiative. How could it be otherwise? We can't avert the wrath of God. We're the problem, not the answer. We're helpless before God. But "God so loved the world, that he gave his only Son . . ." (John 3:16). At the cross, his love satisfied his own wrath. That's the second thing God was setting forth in the death of Christ.

What we couldn't do, God has done. He has made a way for his frown to turn into his smile. The cross didn't make God propitious; the cross was God's idea to begin with. And he did it out in the open, as a fact of history, so that the story could be told over and over again.

What the sacrifice of millions of lambs in the Old Testament could never accomplish, God has done through Christ. He did it out in the open for everyone to see, because God desires your conscience to be set free. The full fury of the wrath of God was unleashed onto a willing substitute at the cross. This is what God put forward so clearly.

Stop believing your own thoughts. Stop brooding over your own guilt. You will never relax and enjoy peace with God. When your sins oppress you, believe something else. Believe the gospel that God himself has made so clear. And every time your heart shrinks from God in dread, believe it all over again. The Bible says, "For freedom Christ has set us free; stand firm therefore and do not submit again to the yoke of slavery" (Gal. 5:1).

My dad told me a story about Donald Grey Barnhouse, who was a Presbyterian minister in the middle of the twentieth century and a hero to my dad. Dr. Barnhouse was waiting to preach in a church. But first someone sang the old song, "I Am Satisfied," which asks the question, "I am satisfied with Christ, but is he satisfied with me?" And when the singer was finished, Dr. Barnhouse stepped into the pulpit and said, "Yes, he is!" God wants us to trade in our own thoughts of how we can prove ourselves to God for new thoughts of how he has proven himself to us. It's the truth. And there is saving power for sinners in this truth.

How do we get in on it? How do we get back inside, again and again? The Scripture says, God put Christ Jesus forward "as a propitiation by his blood, *to be received by faith*." If God presented Jesus as his great statement to you and me, then what's our part? "To be received by faith." The way to experience gospel freedom is by faith. In other words, faith is the set of eyes that notice what God has presented. Faith is the mentality that admires what God has put forward. Faith is the heart that prizes what God has displayed. Faith is the urgency and confidence that runs to it.

Who qualifies to enjoy the liberating power of the death of Christ? Sinners. They're the only people he died for. If your problems are always someone else's fault, if you come to God standing upright and ready to make your own case, the cross condemns you. But if you're far from God, if you've sinned and you keep on sinning and you're ashamed and wish you could trade in your record for a better one, if your conscience knows that you deserve the wrath of God and your only hope is God's mercy in Christ, then he longs for you to know something. He longs for you to know that he is happy over you, because he sees you through the death of Christ. God is not angry at you any more; he rejoices over you. You've got to know that. He longs for you to know that your sins have been nailed to the cross, and you bear them no more.

Adapted from "The Most Important Word in the Universe," sermon by Raymond C. Ortlund Jr., Christ Presbyterian Church, Nashville, September 11, 2005. Used by permission.

Scripture references are from *The Holy Bible: New International Version*®.

21

ℛESURRECTION ℘REVIEW

Francis Schaeffer

"And after six days Jesus took with him Peter and James, and John
his brother, and led them up a high mountain by themselves. And
he was transfigured before them, and his face shone like the sun,
and his clothes became white as light. And behold, there appeared
to them Moses and Elijah, talking with him. And Peter said to Jesus,
'Lord, it is good that we are here. If you wish, I will make three tents
here, one for you and one for Moses and one for Elijah.' He was still
speaking when, behold, a bright cloud overshadowed them, and a
voice from the cloud said, 'This is my beloved Son, with whom I
am well pleased; listen to him.' When the disciples heard this, they
fell on their faces and were terrified. But Jesus came and touched
them, saying, 'Rise, and have no fear.' And when they lifted up their
eyes, they saw no one but Jesus only."

Matthew 17:1–8

any aspects of the transfiguration should make us
marvel. The first wonder of the transfiguration is its
space-timeness. Four men walked up a mountain

to a certain place, a certain point of geography, just as we would walk up a mountain of Switzerland. The clock was ticking; had the men had watches, they could have determined what time it was. Their watches would not have stopped halfway up the mountain. Life was still going on in an unbroken way at the bottom of the mountain. There was no break in either time or space. And right in the middle of the space-time world occurred something that men would think of as supernatural. Suddenly Moses and Elijah appeared (one long dead, one long ago translated), and Jesus was glorified.

This did not occur merely in someone's thought-world. It was not some upper-story situation, where modern theologians would put religious events. Nor was it in an area of a philosophic other. Rather, it was the simplest thing one could imagine, and the most profound: the supernatural occurred in the midst of history. An entire worldview is involved in this one concept.

The second wonder of the transfiguration is that Moses and Elijah were present. Moses had died about 1,500 years before Christ, and about 900 years prior to the birth of Jesus. Elijah had been taken to heaven without dying; and yet here the two men were, not as wisps of vapor but as recognizable forms. In Moses we see what we will be like between our death and the resurrection of our bodies—if Jesus does not come back before we die. Cartoonists love to draw ghosts coming in through keyholes, but this is not the biblical picture of who we are between our death and our resurrection.

The transfiguration gives a preview of the resurrection that believers will experience when Jesus returns.

A three-way conversation could take place (a propositional, verbalized communication that could be understood by the disciples in normal terms) between Moses, who had died, Elijah, who had been translated, and Christ, who had come up the mountainside.

The third wonder of the transfiguration is that it gives a preview of the resurrection that believers will experience when Jesus returns. As Jesus' transfiguration and resurrection were in the midst of space and time, so too the resurrection of Christians will occur in history and will be historic. The word "historic" does not mean "past." It means "space-timeness"—that something will occur or has occurred at a certain tick of the clock and at a certain geographic place.

The real wonder of the transfiguration, however, is Christ himself. The end of the narrative reminds us of its focal point: "And when they had lifted up their eyes, they saw no man, save Jesus only" (Matt. 17:8).

Why Jesus is so important had been revealed to the disciples earlier: "And while he [Jesus] yet spoke, behold, a bright cloud overshadowed them: and behold a voice out of the cloud, which said, This is my beloved Son, in whom I am well pleased; hear ye him" (17:5). The reason the Father said, "Hear him" is that Jesus is deity, the eternal second person of the Trinity. He was, therefore, the center of this whole affair. The center was not Elijah, or Moses, wonderful as their appearance was, or the disciples; the center was Jesus himself.

It is intriguing that Moses, Elijah, and Jesus talked about something. What would you think would be important enough to discuss at such a moment? If we took a poll of people's guesses, I wonder whether any conjecture would be a fit subject for such a titanic moment! However, we need not speculate because Luke tells us they "spake of his decease which he was about to accomplish at Jerusalem" (Luke 9:31). The only subject worthy of conversation at this moment was Jesus' coming death.

Why was this so? Because Moses, Elijah, the disciples, and all the Old and New Testament saints had, and have, a stake in it. If Jesus had not died, everything would have collapsed. Redemption depended on his substitutionary, propitiatory death. If Jesus had not died, if he had turned aside (as Satan tried to make him do so many times), if he had, in Peter's words, actually had pity on himself and not gone on to the cross, everything would have been gone. There would have been no hope for Elijah, translated or not. It would have meant the end of Moses, the disciples, and everyone else, because the redemption of everything depends on the single focus point of Jesus' death. John the Baptist, the last Old Testament prophet, had proclaimed as he introduced Jesus to the Jews, "Behold the Lamb of God, which taketh away the sin of the world" (John 1:29), and no other conversation was big enough for the Mount of Transfiguration. Jesus' resurrection is certainly important. So too are his ascension and his teachings. But the welfare of every believer and the entire creation depends upon his death.

Yes, the real wonder is Christ, the eternal Son of God who came to earth to die, who was glorified on the Mount of Transfiguration. And he "was transfigured before them: and his face did shine as the sun, and his raiment was as white as the light" (Matt. 17:2). We can think of this as the prefiguration of his coming resurrection body.

After his resurrection he had a body that could still be touched and could still eat, but it was changed so that he could move back and forth from the seen to the unseen world, as he did many times in the forty days after his resurrection. He would appear—on the road to Emmaus or in a room—and then no longer be seen. Then Jesus' glorification continued in the ascension when, as an official act, as the conclusion of his earthly ministry, Christ with his resurrected body left the earth.

On the Mount of Transfiguration, in the resurrection, and then in three post-ascension appearances, men saw him as we shall when we see him. In the transfiguration he was glorified, prefiguring what he is like now and what he will be like when we see him in the future face to face.

Excerpted from *No Little People* by Francis Schaeffer. Copyright © 1974 by L'Abri Fellowship. Used by permission of Crossway Books.

Scripture quotations are from the *King James Version* of the Bible.

22

𝔓eace 𝔅e unto 𝔜ou

Saint Augustine

"As they were talking about these things, Jesus himself stood among them, and said to them, 'Peace to you!' But they were startled and frightened and thought they saw a spirit. And he said to them, 'Why are you troubled, and why do doubts arise in your hearts? See my hands and my feet, that it is I myself. Touch me, and see. For a spirit does not have flesh and bones as you see that I have.' And when he had said this, he showed them his hands and his feet. And while they still disbelieved for joy and were marveling, he said to them, 'Have you anything here to eat?' They gave him a piece of broiled fish, and he took it and ate before them. Then he said to them, 'These are my words that I spoke to you while I was still with you, that everything written about me in the Law of Moses and the Prophets and the Psalms must be fulfilled.' Then he opened their minds to understand the Scriptures."

Luke 24:36–45

he Lord appeared to his disciples after his resurrection and saluted them, saying, "Peace be unto you." This is peace indeed, and the salutation of salvation: for the very word "salutation" has received its name from salvation. And what can be better than that salvation itself should salute man? For Christ is our salvation. He is our salvation, who was wounded for us, and fixed by nails to the tree, and being taken down from the tree, was laid in the sepulcher. And from the sepulcher he arose, with his wounds healed, his scars kept. For this he judged expedient for his disciples, that his scars should be kept, whereby the wounds of their hearts might be healed. What wounds? The wounds of unbelief. For he appeared to their eyes, exhibiting real flesh, and they thought they saw a spirit. It is no light wound, this wound of the heart. Yea, they have made a malignant heresy who have abided in this wound. But do we suppose that the disciples had not been wounded, because they were so quickly healed? Only, beloved, suppose, if they had continued in this wound, to think that the body which had been buried, could not rise again, but that a spirit in the image of a body, deceived the eyes of men. If they had continued in this belief, yea, rather in this unbelief, not their wounds, but their death would have had to be bewailed.

But what said the Lord Jesus? "Why are ye troubled, and why do thoughts ascend into your hearts?" (Luke 24:38). If thoughts ascend into your heart, the thoughts come from the earth. But it is good for a man, not that a thought should ascend into his heart, but that his heart should itself ascend upward, where the apostle would have believers place their hearts, to whom he said, "If ye be risen with Christ, mind those things which are above, where Christ is sitting at the right hand of God. Seek those things which are above, not the things which are upon the earth. For ye are dead, and your life is hid with Christ in God. When Christ your life shall appear, then shall ye also appear with Him in glory" (Col. 3:1–4). In what glory? The glory of the resurrection. In what glory? Hear the apostle saying of this body, "It is sown in dishonour, it shall rise in glory" (1 Cor. 15:43). This glory the apostles were unwilling to assign to their Master, their Christ, their Lord; they did not believe that his body could rise from the sepulcher; they thought him to be a Spirit, though they saw his flesh, and they believed not their very eyes. Malignant wound! Let the remedies for these scars come forth. "Why are ye troubled, and why do thoughts ascend into your hearts? See My hands and My feet," where I was fixed with the nails. "Handle and see." Ye see, and yet do not see. "Handle and see" what? "That a spirit hath not flesh and bones, as ye see me have." So it is written, "When he had thus spoken, He showed them His hands and His feet" (Luke 24:40).

From the sepulcher he arose, with his wounds healed, his scars kept . . . whereby the wounds of their hearts might be healed.

"And while they were yet in hesitation, and wondered for joy" (Luke 24:41). Now there was joy already, and yet hesitation continued. For a thing incredible had taken place, yet taken place it had. Is it at this day a thing incredible, that the body of the Lord rose again from the sepulcher? The whole cleansed world has believed it; whoso has not believed it has remained in his uncleanness. Yet at that time it was incredible; and persuasion was addressed not to the eyes only, but to the hands also, that by the bodily senses faith might descend into their heart, and that faith so descending into their heart might be preached throughout the world to them who neither saw nor touched, and yet without doubting believed. "Have ye," saith he, "anything to eat?" How much doeth the good builder still to build up the edifice of faith? He did not hunger, yet he asked to eat. And he ate by an act of his power, not through necessity. So then let the disciples acknowledge the verity of his body, which the world has acknowledged at their preaching.

If haply there be any heretics who still in their hearts maintain that Christ exhibited himself to sight, but that Christ's was not very flesh, let them now lay aside that error, and let the gospel persuade them. We do but blame them for entertaining this conceit; he will damn them if they shall persevere in it. Who art thou who dost not believe that a body laid in the sepulchre could rise again? If thou art a Manichee, who dost not believe that he was crucified either, because thou dost not believe that he was even born, thou declarest that all that he showed was false. He showed what was false, and dost thou speak the truth? Thou dost not lie with thy mouth, and did he lie in his body? Lo thou dost suppose that he appeared unto the eyes of men what he really was not, that he was a spirit, not flesh. Hear him; he loves thee, let him not condemn thee. Hear him speaking; lo, he speaks to thee, thou unhappy one, he speaks to thee: "Why art thou troubled, and why do thoughts ascend into thine heart?" "See," saith he, "My hands and My feet. Handle and see, because a spirit hath not flesh and bones as ye see Me have." This spake the truth, and did he deceive? It was a body then, it was flesh; that which had been buried, appeared. Let doubting perish, and meet praise ensue.

Come then, O Lord, employ thy keys, open, that we may understand. Lo, thou dost tell all things, and yet are not believed. Thou art thought to be a spirit, art touched, art rudely handled, and yet they who touch thee hesitate. Thou dost admonish them out of the Scriptures, and yet they understand thee not. Their hearts are closed. Open and enter in. Open, O Lord, yea, open the heart of him who is in doubt concerning Christ. Open his understanding who believes that Christ was a phantom. "Then opened He their understanding, that they might understand the Scriptures."

Adapted from *St. Augustine: Homilies on the Gospels* in *The Nicene and Post-Nicene Fathers*, First Series, vol. 6, edited by Philip Schaff, Sermon LXVI (CXVI. Ben.).

23

KNOWING THE POWER OF HIS RESURRECTION

Tim Keller

"But whatever gain I had, I counted as loss for the sake of Christ. Indeed, I count everything as loss because of the surpassing worth of knowing Christ Jesus my Lord. For his sake I have suffered the loss of all things and count them as rubbish, in order that I may gain Christ and be found in him, not having a righteousness of my own that comes from the law, but that which comes through faith in Christ, the righteousness from God that depends on faith—that I may know him and the power of his resurrection, and may share his sufferings, becoming like him in his death, that by any means possible I may attain the resurrection from the dead."

Philippians 3:7–11

 was watching a documentary recently on PBS and there was a minister who was asked, "Do you believe Jesus was raised from the dead?" And he responded, "The purpose and the personality and the power that was in Jesus continues, so that today he is a risen and living presence and possibility." What was he saying? He was suggesting that the purpose of Jesus lives on but that he is still physically dead.

On one hand, the resurrection is a fact to be believed. On the other hand, it is an experience to connect with.

But if Jesus' example lives on while he is really dead, you can only know him as an example. You can't talk to him, and he can't talk to you. If Jesus is not really living, he is not a living force who can come in and intervene in your life. You will have a form of religion without any power.

But on the other hand, it is also possible to be orthodox about your belief in the resurrection of Jesus, but if you've never had a profound experience of that resurrection, your own spiritual resurrection, then you have a form of religion without power as well.

On one hand, the resurrection is a fact to be believed. On the other hand, it is an experience to connect with. If you have one without the other—if you believe in the resurrection as historical fact but never experience the resurrection personally, or if you think of the resurrection as a spiritual experience but don't believe it was a fact—you come out with a form of religion with no power.

My question is: *Do you know them both? Do you believe in the resurrection as a historical event, and have you also had that profound personal experience of spiritual resurrection?* Christianity refuses to be stuck in either category. It is not all about rationality, nor is it all about mysticism. It's both. On one hand, Christianity is about beliefs, proposition, and ethics. But that's not enough. You have to experience him to know him. There has to be a real connection. And on the other hand, Christianity is not only a mystical religion. It's not like Eastern religions with no rational content. Christianity has hard edges to it. It says, "This is true, and this is false. This will get you saved. This will get you damned. This actually happened."

Christianity says that if you want to experience God, you have to believe the truth. You have to believe that he really lived, that he really died, that he was really raised. And if you see that truth and believe in it, it leads to an experience, which leads to more understanding of the truth, and the truth leads to more experience.

This week I saw a dog—a big dog—who wanted something to eat. The dog was on a leash attached to a collar that had a choke chain on it. The chain would bite into his neck to keep him from pulling on the leash. And yet he strained against the leash, because he saw food that he wanted. He wanted the food more than he didn't want to experience the pain. He had one ambition—to get the meat. The pain was secondary. So he strained against the leash and let it bite in.

This is the kind of passion and ambition Paul describes in Philippians 3 when he says that he has counted all things as loss so that he can gain Christ. Paul says even though he loved all those things, he has a great ambition. He wants to know Christ and the power of his resurrection.

To be a Christian is not just to believe in a set of propositions. It is that, but it's much more. It is to say, "I count everything as loss or rubbish in comparison to my number one ambition, which is to know Christ and the power of his resurrection and the fellowship of sharing in his suffering." Paul is saying that if you understand the doctrine of the resurrection you don't just believe, you have a passion.

A person with a passion for Christ is not necessarily always talking about Christ, but is looking at everything through Christ.

When I talk about having a passion for Christ, it might make you afraid that I mean you need to be a fanatic. Maybe you think, *I had an aunt like that. All she did was*

talk about religion and the Bible and made everybody sick of it.
That's not what we're talking about when we talk about a passion
for Christ.

It's like my glasses. I don't spend all my time looking at and
talking about my glasses. But I do spend all my time seeing everything through my glasses. And if my relationship between me and
my glasses gets off, if they get too far down on my nose or get too
dirty, it affects my perception of everything.

Likewise, a person with a passion for Christ is not necessarily
always talking *about* Christ, but is looking at everything *through*
Christ.

So how does a person with a passion for Christ deal with worry?
You go to Jesus. You look at your concerns through the perspective
of Christ. How do you deal with bitterness? You look at how Christ
has forgiven you. How do you deal with fear? You take it to Jesus.
How do you decide how much money to spend in a year on what
items? You go to Jesus. You look at his teachings. You think about
things through his values.

For the person with a passion for Christ, Christ is like your
glasses. You're not necessarily always seeing Christ, but you're
seeing everything through him.

Do you strain with all of your might to see things the way Christ
sees them? Do you strain to please him in everything? Do you
strain to understand everything through him? Do you have that
passion, or do you just believe the propositions?

I was reading the other day about a man who lived one hundred
years ago who wrote a friend:

Recently as I've been having great times in prayer, usually once a
week and sometimes once a day, a pressure of his great love comes
down upon my heart, in such measure as makes my whole being
groan beneath the joy. He hath unlocked every apartment of my

being and filled and flooded them with his presence. The inner spot is being touched, and all my flintiness is being melted.

It's one thing to believe that Jesus loves you in a general way. It's another thing to have his love come down. That's what it means to know Christ. Have you experienced that, or do you just say your prayers? Has his love come down and touched the inner spot?

Religious people are very busy in their religion doing lots of religious activities, and then they expect their lives to go the way they want them to go. And if they find their career or their love life isn't going very well, they say, "What good is all this religion? I'm doing all these things, where's God?"

But what a Christian says is, "If trouble in my love life has helped me to know Christ, if a lack of success in my career helps me know him better, then great. I count it all as rubbish because the surpassing thing is to know him."

Paul not only has a passion to know Christ; he says he wants to know the power of his resurrection. The difference between knowing Christ and knowing the power of his resurrection is the difference between knowing a person and resembling a person.

To know Christ is to interact with him personally. But the power of his resurrection is the very life energy that took his dead body and raised it up to life again. So for me to know the power of his resurrection is to have the same power that came into Jesus and raised him up to come into my dead soul and raise me up. This is not about relationship but about supernatural character growth. When Paul says, "I want to know him," it means, "I want to be with him," but when he says, "I want to know the power of his resurrection," it means, "I want to be just like him."

Look at the deadness in your life. Look at the anger. How is that going to be turned into forgiveness? Look at the insecurity. How is that going to be turned into confidence? Look at the self-centeredness. How is that going to be turned into compassion and generosity? How? The answer is that the dead stuff gets taken over by the Spirit of God.

Many people believe the propositions. They believe the historical facts about Jesus, but their real agenda is personal success. So they go to Christ when they want to and need to. Paul says that a Christian is someone who has turned that all around so that personal success is defined by knowing him and the power of his resurrection, and everything else becomes second.

The minute you decide to receive Jesus as Savior and Lord, the power of the Holy Spirit comes into your life. It's the power of the resurrection—the same thing that raised Jesus from the dead.

A minister was in Italy, and there he saw the grave of a man who had died centuries before who was an unbeliever and completely against Christianity, but a little afraid of it too. So the man had a huge stone slab put over his grave so he would not have to be raised from the dead in case there is a resurrection from the dead. He had insignias put all over the slab saying, "I do not want to be raised form the dead. I don't believe in it." Evidently, when he was buried, an acorn must have fallen into the grave. So a hundred years later the acorn had grown up through the grave and split that slab. It was now a tall towering oak tree. The minister looked at it and asked, "If an acorn, which has power of biological life in it, can split a slab of that magnitude, what can the acorn of God's resurrection power do in a person's life?"

Think of the things you see as immovable slabs in your life—your bitterness, your insecurity, your fears, your self-doubts. Those things can be split and rolled off. The more you know him, the more you grow into the power of the resurrection. The more time you spend with him, seek him, read his Word, the more you pray—the more it stirs up the resurrection power that is within you through the Holy Spirit.

There is one more thing Paul says here that he wants: "I want to know the fellowship of sharing in his sufferings." Some would say this doesn't make sense. To know the power of his resurrection and share in his sufferings, what does it mean?

It's perfectly logical. If you go out into the world resembling Jesus by his resurrection power within you—if you turn the other cheek, if you love people who are unlovable, if you always tell the truth—what will happen? You will find his sufferings reenacted in your life. People are going to be unhappy with you. You'll be taken advantage of. People will be offended. If they were offended by Jesus, why wouldn't they be offended by you if you resemble Jesus?

Jesus said, "I am the resurrection and the life. He who believes in me will live, even though he dies; and whoever lives and believes in me will never die . . ." (John 11:25–26). He was saying: The one who unites with me by faith becomes spiritually alive and is transformed from one degree of splendor to the next, and the process goes on and on forever and even physical death can't stop it. Death actually moves this process on to perfection.

When the body dies, our spirits burst into flame in his presence, and we burn bright with his energy, power, and goodness—all of his glory flowing in and out of us. That's what we're in for. We'll be like him, and his resurrection power will be complete in us.

24

SHARING HIS SUFFERINGS
Joni Eareckson Tada

"That I may know him and the power of his resurrection, and may share his sufferings, becoming like him in his death."

Philippians 3:10

When do I get to have my wheelchair, Daddy?" Five-year-old Matthew looked up into the face of his father, his liquid brown eyes doleful and pleading. Matthew and his brother, Stephen, had spent a week with their parents volunteering at one of our Joni and Friends Retreats. They made buddies with scores of boys and girls who used crutches, walkers, and wheelchairs. I laughed when Jim, their father, relayed to me Matthew's request. This little boy doesn't need a wheelchair. He has no use for one. But try telling him that!

A wheelchair, for Matthew, would top his Christmas wish list. A wheelchair means a joy ride. It also means an initiation into a wonderful club: a special group of kids who enjoy a special relationship with Joni. This five-year-old hasn't a clue about the pain and paralysis, the heartaches and hurdles. He discounts all of that, disregarding the dark side. All he desires is a chance to be among

God delights in identifying with us in our suffering. . . . He feels the sting in his chest when you hurt. He takes it personally.

my best friends, a chance to identify with me, be like me, a chance to know me. If it means having a wheelchair, great. He'll welcome it.

It takes a child like Matthew to illuminate the true emotion behind the apostle Paul's words, "I consider everything a loss compared to the surpassing greatness of knowing Christ Jesus my Lord, for whose sake I have lost all things. I consider them rubbish, that I may gain Christ and be found in him. . . . I want

to know Christ and the power of his resurrection and the fellowship of sharing in his sufferings, becoming like him in his death" (Phil. 3:8–10).

Matthew wanted to join a club, but the fellowship of Christ's sufferings is not an inner circle of elite believers. The word fellowship in the original text was *koinonia*—the experience of sharing something in common.

God delights in identifying with us in our suffering. When the apostle Paul was on the road to Damascus, the risen Lord didn't say, "Saul, why are you persecuting my people?" God said, "Why are you persecuting *me*?" (see Acts 9:4). He considers our sufferings his sufferings. He feels the sting in his chest when you hurt. He takes it personally.

Jesus is a Savior who can "sympathize with our weaknesses . . . one who has been tempted in every way, just as we are—yet was without sin" (Heb. 4:15). My blind friend Peter shares how humiliated he was when, as a teenager, he fell after striking his head on a low branch. Sprawled on the ground in front of his friends, he felt hurt and embarrassed. His confidence in God was shaken: *You don't understand what it's like to be blind, God. To not know where the next blow might come from!* But Jesus does. "The men who were guarding Jesus began mocking and beating him. They blindfolded him and demanded, 'Prophesy! Who hit you?'" (Luke 22:63–64).

Another friend, Gloria, fell into deep anguish over the dismal prognosis of her daughter's illness. Little Laura had already suffered enough from the degenerative nerve disorder she had been born with, and now the doctors' forecast included more suffering and impending death. One night after leaving her daughter's bedside, she spat, "God, it's not right. You've never had to watch one of your children die!" As soon as the words escaped, she clasped her hand over her mouth. He did watch his child die. His one and only Son.

The invitation to know God— really know him—is always an invitation to suffer. Not to suffer alone, but to suffer with him.

Early on when I realized Jesus is a Savior who could sympathize with our weakness, I was passionately telling everybody how "Christ was paralyzed on the cross," how he understood how I felt. A stressed-out firefighter happened to cross the wake of my enthusiasm. In the diner where we met, I offered, "He's been there. He understands." Outside, taxis honked and trucks rumbled by, but we were oblivious. The fireman's gaze held mine—me, cheerful and sincere; he, disbelieving and with scorn lining his tired mouth. "So he understands. Big deal. What good does that do me?" he bristled as he raised his arms from under the table. His rolled-up sleeves revealed the smooth ends of two stumps where hands should be. "Burned off in a blaze. Lost my job."

I was taken aback. I was fresh out of the hospital and certainly no theology student or expert on the Bible. Cheer drained from my face. I answered as honestly as I knew how. "I don't know all the answers. And I'm not sure if I did that it would help. But I do know the One who has the answers." A long pause. His gaze lowered. "And knowing him makes all the difference." I had never spoken with such confidence, but I sensed the *espirit de corps* with this man with no hands. I then shocked myself by saying for the first time since my accident, "I'd rather be in this chair knowing him than on my feet without him."

The fireman didn't need a briefcase full of words. He needed the Word. The Word made flesh—gouged, with nail-pierced wrists, hands nearly ripped off. Spat upon, beaten bloody, with flies buzzing and hatred hammering. These aren't merely facts about Jesus. This isn't love as an abstract idea. This is love poured out like wine as strong as fire. In that diner, the fireman stopped thinking of God as a meditating mystic on a faraway mountain. No longer was he an abstract deity. Nothing neat and tidy about him. God got messy when he smeared his blood on a cross to save people from hellfire. This held a strange appeal for this man who had injured himself rescuing others from the flames.

Programs, systems, and methods sit well in the ivory towers of monasteries or in the wooden arms of icons. Head knowledge comes from the pages of a theology text. But the invitation to know God—really know him—is always an invitation to suffer. Not to suffer alone, but to suffer with him. "If anyone would come after me, he must deny himself and take up his cross and follow me. For whoever wants to save his life will lose it, but whoever loses his life for me and for the gospel will save it" (Mark 8:34–35).

The fireman was gripped. God didn't merely expose the fireman's sin, he entered it. He came into it. Like entering a burning building to hand a baby out the window just in the nick of time. But Jesus lost more than his hand; he lost his life. Thankfully, he was not scorched by death. He burst back to life. What power! If I'm to be held steady in the midst of my suffering, I want to be held not by a doctrine or a cause but by the most powerful Person in the universe.

Amazing love, how can it be? That God should plunge the knife in his heart for me—all the while, me, dry and indifferent, cool and detached. That he, the God of life, should conquer death by embracing it. That he should destroy the power of sin by letting it destroy him.

25

CRUCIFIED WITH CHRIST

Stephen F. Olford

"I have been crucified with Christ. It is no longer I who live, but Christ who lives in me. And the life I now live in the flesh I live by faith in the Son of God, who loved me and gave himself for me."

Galatians 2:20

"I have been crucified with Christ" (Gal. 2:20). This glorious truth changed the life of Martin Luther, John Calvin, all the great Reformers, and simple Christians down through the centuries. When Paul says, "I have been crucified with Christ," he is restating what he has affirmed in his Roman epistle: "For what the law could not do in that it was weak through the flesh, God did by sending His own Son in the likeness of sinful flesh, on account of sin: *He condemned sin in the flesh,* that the righteous requirement of the law might be fulfilled in us who do not walk according to the flesh but according to the Spirit" (Rom. 8:3–4).

The self-life is sin in the flesh, and God has condemned it. When the Lord Jesus Christ came, he not only embodied and expounded the Law, but he *exacted* the Law. He exacted it by taking the penalty of your sin and my sin at Calvary and paying our sin debt on the cross. So he condemned sin in the flesh. Anyone who tries to perfect the flesh, which is the humanistic view in our religious world today, is violating the very truth of God. But what God condemns, he crucifies.

"Knowing this, that our old man was crucified with Him, that the body of sin might be done away with, that we should no longer be slaves of sin" (Rom. 6:6). The crucified life is an important doctrine. If we do not accept our crucifixion, how can we accept our resurrection in Christ? One of the great truths that has transformed my life is the fact that "Christ died for our sins according to the Scriptures, and that He was buried, and that He rose again the third day according to the Scriptures" (1 Cor. 15:3–4).

Soon after I understood this message, I went out to preach, but the Devil kept saying to me, "Stephen, how can you dare preach the victorious life? Just think back a few years to your backsliding days and the dreadful life you lived then." The Devil paralyzed me; he shut my mouth; he silenced my witness.

But in my distress I went to hear a missionary who was expounding the early chapters of the Roman epistle. He came to chapter 6 and said, "I wonder if there is a young man here this evening who once had a glowing testimony, but now you are totally paralyzed. You are obsessed with introspection, and the Devil is saying to you, 'You know what you were. What a hypocrite you are to open your mouth now.'" Then this dear man of God, in the flow of his message, pointed his finger at the audience and said, "Beloved young man, if you are sitting here tonight, I want to tell you that you are violating the law of Romans 6. You were buried! What God condemns, he crucifies. What God crucifies, he buries. What is buried, *you are not to dig up.*"

As I heard those words, God set me free! I saw the truth that Christ died for me; I died with him. He went to the grave, and so did I. On the basis of that death and burial, I can claim resurrection life! If you want to know Christ's resurrection power released in you, then sincerely pray, "Lord, I am dead, but alive in you. Resurrection power, fill me this hour. Jesus, be Jesus in me.'" This is the termination of the self-life.

Romans 8:13 gives an exposition of this doctrine of the crucified life. "For if you live according to the flesh," that is, the self-life, "you will die. . . ." Everything you touch will die. Your preaching will die, your praying will die, your quiet time will die, and your witnessing will die. But if by the Spirit you put to death (go on putting to death, present tense) the deeds of the body, you will live.

You cannot crucify yourself; it is one death that you cannot self-inflict. You have to be crucified.

This is a clear distinction between biblical crucifixion and self-mutilation. You do not have to go to a monastery in order to mutilate yourself! That is not what the Bible says. You cannot crucify yourself; it is one death that *you cannot self-inflict*. You have *to be crucified*. That is exactly how the Lord Jesus died. But before bowing his head and dying with power, he cried victoriously, "It is finished!" (John 19:30). "He was crucified in weakness" (2 Cor. 13:4). Contradiction? No. Paul is explaining that when Christ came to Golgotha, he did not struggle. Instead, he gave his hands to be crucified, he gave his feet to be crucified, he gave himself to be crucified. How did he do that? He "through the eternal Spirit offered Himself without spot" to be crucified (Heb. 9:14).

How am I to be crucified? By the same Spirit. So as I live my life moment by moment and sense self rearing its ugly head, I count on the Holy Spirit to put to death the deeds of the body (Rom. 8:12–15). Crucifixion is not an *instantaneous* death. It's a lingering death till Jesus comes. A thousand times a day I have to say, "Lord Jesus, I sense self rising." I have a "little radar" that the Lord has put in my life! The radar catches the vibes from self. It may be that I have said an unkind word to my wife. It may be that I have rebuked my children without the spirit of love. It may be that I have taken glory to myself when someone praises me. I say, "Holy Spirit, nail it." And that is precisely what he does. Self goes to the cross where self belongs, and Jesus comes through my personality in all the glory of his presence and power.

Excerpted from *The Way of Holiness* by Stephen F. Olford. Copyright © 1998 by Stephen F. Olford. Used by permission of Crossway Books.

Scripture references are from *The New King James Version*.

Grant me more and more of the resurrection life:
    may it rule me,
    may I walk in its power,
    and be strengthened through its influence.
                —The Valley of Vision

NOTES

Chapter 3: An Innocent Man Crushed by God
1. "How Great Thou Art," Stuart K. Hine, 1949.
2. "Man of Sorrows! What a Name," Philip P. Bliss, 1875.

Chapter 4: The Cup
1. William Lane, *Commentary on the Gospel of Mark* (Grand Rapids, MI: Eerdmans, 1974), 516.

Chapter 5: Gethsemane
1. William Barclay, *The Gospel of John* (Philadelphia: Westminster, 1956), 2:259.
2. T. H. L. Parker, trans., *The Gospel According to St. John* (Grand Rapids, MI: Eerdmans, 1974), 5:156.

Chapter 6: Betrayed, Denied, Deserted
1. William Hendriksen, *Exposition of the Gospel According to John*, New Testament Commentary (1953; repr., Grand Rapids: Baker, 2002), 378.
2. J. C. Ryle, *Expository Thoughts on the Gospels*, vol. 1: *Matthew* (1879; repr., Grand Rapids: Baker, 1977), 369.
3. J. C. Ryle, *Matthew*, Crossway Classic Commentaries, eds. Alister McGrath and J. I. Packer (Wheaton, IL: Crossway, 1993), 266.

Chapter 10: Father, Forgive Them
1. J. C. Ryle, *Expository Thoughts on the Gospels*, vol. 2: *Luke* (1879; repr., Grand Rapids: Baker, 1977), 467.

Chapter 13: I Am Thirsty

1. C. S. Lewis, *The Great Divorce* (New York: Macmillan, 1946), 72.

Chapter 14: God-Forsaken

1. J. Blinzler, *The Trial of Jesus* (Westminster, MD: Newman, 1959), 261.

Chapter 18: He Descended into Hell and Ascended into Heaven

1. C. S. Lewis, *Miracles: A Preliminary Study* (New York: Macmillan, 1947), 186.

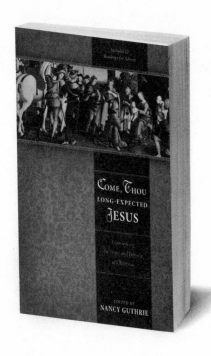

"And the Word became flesh and dwelt among us, and we have seen his glory, glory as of the only Son from the Father, full of grace and truth."

Now Available

This special anthology of advent readings, collected from the works of 22 classic and contemporary theologians and Bible teachers with a high view of Scripture, will awaken your longing for a fresh experience of the coming of Jesus and prepare your heart to honor the sacredness of each Christmas season.

Includes selections from the works and sermons of classic theologians such as Whitefield, Spurgeon, and Augustine, and from leading contemporary communicators such as John Piper, Randy Alcorn, and Francis Schaeffer.